THE DAY
THE DOLLAR DIES

WILLARD CANTELON

LOGOS INTERNATIONAL, Plainfield, New Jersey

THE DAY THE DOLLAR DIES
© 1973 Logos International, Plainfield, N.J. 07060
All Rights Reserved
Printed in the United States of America
Library of Congress Catalog Card Number: 72-94186
ISBN: 0-88270-013-8

Contents

Foreword

BERLIN was in shambles, Frankfurt and Stuttgart in ruins. Millions of refugees wandered the streets of West German cities where the ghostly remains of bombed buildings stared without sympathy at the homeless seeking shelter.

The war was over, but the wounds remained. They would take time to heal.

Years would be required to remove the rubble, and memories of Adolph Hitler would never be erased. Germany's rebuilding would require more than brick and mortar. Faith once firm in the hearts of older Germans had been severely shaken by 19 years of Nazi domination.

On the edge of Frankfurt, I stood with a friend, J. P. Kolenda. Together we stared at the squat gray buildings surrounded by tall grass and weeds.

"So you plan to establish a school in this place to train young Germans for the ministry," I said slowly.

"I know the buildings are drab and inadequate," replied my friend. "We would build better if we had the funds."

Slowly I reached out my hand and shook his in agreement. Then for a moment I stared at my hand, as if it belonged to someone other than myself. Why had I pledged my help so impulsively? How much money would I have to raise? And where? And how?

The weeks that followed my commitment at Frankfurt were rainy ones. The skies of Germany continued to mourn the millions of lives lost in the war.

On the rain-soaked hills of Württemberg we gathered together an unusual group of men. There was a platoon of special police who, at our request, had donned uniforms resembling the SS guards of the Third Reich. Then there were the two pathetic-looking figures who stood shackled and blindfolded, awaiting execution. Next to me stood my closest friend and cameraman, Colonel Alfred Garr.

The rain stopped falling. I shouted, "Scene 1, Take 1," and we began shooting the final scene of our film, *Three Germanys*. The film would portray the old Germany of the past, war-torn Germany, and a rebuilt Germany. Hopefully, the film would be as acceptable as the first documentaries we had done in India and Africa.

Later that year, the film won not only a film-festival award, but the hearts of the viewers, and proved valuable in raising the needed funds for the German ministerial school.

No scene in the film, however, was as dramatic or sobering as the expression on the face of a little German mother who viewed the film on a special occasion. Moved with a desire to assist the German school, she brought a gift of 10,000 marks for the building program. She held her money with pride and tenderness, as though it was part of her very life. And in a very literal sense, it was exactly that; she had earned the money with the sweat of her brow, and had guarded it constantly in war's destructive years. Now she was investing it in a worthy cause and she beamed with pride as she offered her contribution.

How could I tell her she had held this money too long? Why did it fall my lot to shock this sensitive soul with the news that her money was virtually worthless? Why had she not read the morning paper, or heard the announcement that the new government at Bonn had canceled this currency?

If I told her the truth, how would she react? The *Stars and Stripes*, official paper of the Occupation Forces in Europe, would later list the staggering number of German suicides on that June Sunday in 1948. Millions of Germans were aware that their marks were inflated, but few realized that they were to be so suddenly canceled altogether. Marks that would have bought a house on Saturday would not be sufficient in value to buy a winter coat on Sunday.

"Madam," I said slowly, "I'm awfully sorry, but I cannot accept your money."

"And why not?" she asked, perplexity written on her face.

"Because it has been canceled," I said, as gently as I could.

"But, how could then cancel it? And why?" she cried with dismay.

In those two words rested two great questions! How? and Why? It was not possible in a single sentence to give this honest heart the answer to her questions, but there were longer answers that could be given to her, and to anyone who cared to listen—how and why money was canceled in the past, and would again be canceled in the future.

Early in life, I had become interested in money. Not in possessing it, but in understanding its power, its influence, its origin, and its destiny. Why did the German mark become so inflated in 1923 that it took a wagonload to buy a frankfurter? Why did Hitler blame the Jews for much of Germany's economic woes and destroy millions at Auschwitz and Dachau? Why was the German mark again canceled in June of 1948? Why, with World War II behind us by a quarter of a century, is the Western world now talking daily about a new money system? If a new system would shortly be established, who would control it?

In my early youth, I had been given copies of the documents entitled, *The Protocols of the Learned Elders of Zion*. These articles supposedly contained the plot of a few men representing the financial wizards of the world, who not only controlled the financial resources of men and nations, but planned to control completely every man and nation through monopoly of the world's finances.

With awakened interest, I found myself researching the works of anyone who wrote on the subject, and listening to every speaker who spoke on this theme.

I was amazed to learn that many leaders in government both at home and abroad firmly believed that there was a small group of international bankers – totally different in nature and office from the men who served the public in smaller private banks – who were responsible for setting up and removing kings and financing wars throughout history. These men were frequently referred to as the *Illuminati,* or the Luciferian Society, because they received their power and wisdom directly from Lucifer, the prince of this world.

Extreme as it sounded, I was amazed at the ever-increasing reference to such a society and to the growing general acceptance of the idea of a world government.

While reading *Great Ideas Today: 1971* (published by the *Encyclopaedia Britannica*), I was surprised to find so much of this volume devoted to world government. Space was given to the writings of Dostoevsky, who refers to Christ returning to earth, and being rejected by those who had pledged their loyalties to Lucifer. They were promised by Lucifer that they would be given his wisdom and power, and with him rule mankind.

As I traveled from country to country and studied the trends toward a world government, I saw two forces at work. On one hand, I saw honest and sincere men who felt that only a world government under the control of a strong leader could save the world from poisoning itself through pollution, from famine brought on by exploding population, and from the danger of annihilation by atomic war. These men worked feverishly for the establishment of a world government under the banner of humanitarianism, or concern for man's survival. Along with these, there were also the honest men who daily struggled in the world of finance where world trade had far outgrown the volume of money available, men frustrated by the inadequacies of the old money systems that had their origins in the medieval centuries.

Apart from these honest and sincere men, however, I was forced to the conclusion that there was a small group of men who seemed indeed to be endowed with almost supernatural power, who worked behind the scenes making the key economic — and therefore directive — decisions of many countries. For instance, one of the world's most powerful banking dynasties sprung up in Europe under the name of Rothschild. Its center was in Frankfurt, Germany. On scores of occasions, I had stood in the heart of Frankfurt, gazing up at the mammoth banking houses rising high into the sky. These were tied in a very real and powerful manner to other great banking houses of the world.

In my youth, it seemed that the skylines of the cities were dominated by the church spires pointing heavenward. Now, in every town and city, it was the bank buildings that towered over all else. They seemed like temples indeed, temples built by men who had chosen to serve not God but Mammon.

I determined that I would learn not merely how a world government would be formed, and how a new world money system would be established, but also why.

The subject was not one that could be mastered in a 4- or 7-year span of study at an institution of higher learning. All over the world, each new day brought new developments and broader fulfillments of what men of old declared through inspiration would be fulfilled in our day.

I am humbly grateful to God for the opportunities He has given me to pursue this subject for many years in many places, writing books, producing films, delivering messages.

I am especially grateful for a girl, once known to her Philadelphia friends as Verna Jones.

I met her at the close of a month of meetings in the old Metropolitan Opera House in Philadelphia over a quarter of a century ago. After a 20-minute conversation and 6 months of prayer, I gave her an engagement ring. We were married in Philadelphia on a Saturday, I spoke in Chicago the next day and have missed very few days speaking publicly since. The honorariums from speaking engagements have cared for the family and enabled me to keep us together. Even when our sons, Lee and Paul, were babies, Verna kept them with us in our journeys over continents and oceans.

One day recently in Brussels, my friend, Charles Greenaway, was quoting our mutual friend, J. Philip Hogan.

"There's only one girl in all the wide world who could be happily married to a man like Willard," he said. "Any morning of the week, he may announce at breakfast time, 'We're going to move,' and Verna's reply would usually be the same, 'When? This morning or this afternoon?' "

Thus was I ideally equipped for a quest that would take me into the council chambers of a dozen foreign lands — and into the mentality of the international banker as an archetype.

Willard Cantelon
Glendale, California

1

The Search

MY SEARCH to know the how and why of an impending new world money system took me to the halls of the United Nations and to the galleries of the U.S. Senate. It took me to the capitals of Europe, where we viewed the economic scene through the eyes of the Gnomes of Zurich. And to Brussels, where I listened to the world's leading voices describe a new number system which would soon replace the gold and silver and the currencies of the hour. Frequently, I heard advocates of the new money system lauding its virtues and extolling its advantages over the old systems. But in my mind there always remained one great question: If the new system *was* universal, who would control it?

This was a question of supreme importance. If I believed the pages of history and the statements made by leaders of yesterday, then surely I must believe that those who controlled money would play a major role in the affairs of men.

Britain's Leaders

Reginald McKenna, who had served as Chancellor of England's Exchequer, said in January, 1924,

I am afraid that the ordinary citizen will not like to be told that the banks can and do create money, and they who control the credit of a nation direct the policy of the governments and hold in the hollow of their hands, the destiny of the people.

Sir Drummond Fraser, vice-president of the Institute of Bankers, also stated in 1924,

The Governor of the Bank of England must be the autocrat who dictates the terms upon which alone the government can obtain money.

Lord Gladstone, who also served as Chancellor of Britain's Exchequer, said in 1852,

The government . . . in the matters of finance was to leave the money power supreme and unquestioned.

America's Leaders

President James Garfield said in 1881,

He who controls the money of a nation controls the nation.

Vice-President John Garner said in 1933 in referring to international bankers,

You see, gentlemen, who owns the United States.

Congressman Charles Lindbergh of Minnesota said in 1920,

Financial panics are scientifically created.

An International Banker

In the book entitled, *The Federal Reserve Bank* by H. S. Kenan, Meyer Amschel Rothschild is quoted as saying,

Give me control over a nation's economy, and I care not who writes its laws.

The Father of Communism

In his *Communist Manifesto,* Karl Marx declared,

Money plays the largest part in determining the course of history.

Leaders of the Common Market

In Brussels, I listened to the leaders of Europe's Common Market declare their intentions and plans to establish a new money system replacing the old. What then would be the fate of the present currencies of the Western world when they would be replaced with a new number system?

Would there be a rash of suicides and a cry of despair from the lips of millions, as there was when the stock market crashed in 1929, or when the German mark was canceled in 1948?

Anxiety of Americans Today

Today, Americans are anxious about their future security. They long to know the future. In the November, 1970, issue of *Today's Health,* published by the American Medical Association, reference was made to the

40 million Americans pay 200 million dollars annually to 5,000 astrologers in seeking to know the future.

The interest in astrology continues to increase. 1,200 of the 1,750 newspapers in America carry astrology columns.

60% of the nation professes to believe in witchcraft. In one year alone, Americans purchased over 2,000,000 Ouija boards.

Christ Warned against False Prophets

There shall arise . . . false prophets, and . . . they shall deceive. . . . Behold, I have told you before.

(Matt. 24:24–25)

The Bible Tells Men They Can Know the Future

The prophet Isaiah declared God's message in strong language:

> I am God and there is none like me, Declaring the end from the beginning, and from ancient times the things that are not yet done, saying, My counsel shall stand.
> (Isa. 46:9–10)

The apostle Peter declared,

> We have also a more sure word of prophecy; whereunto ye do well that ye take heed, as unto a light that shineth in a dark place.   (II Pet. 1:19)

Some people not fully conversant with the writings of the prophets of the Bible suggest that they predicted only gloom and doom. But actually, their voices unite in predicting a day of ultimate peace and prosperity.

They are in complete agreement that there will be a day of order and justice when wars cease and there dawns a golden age of world harmony. As man approaches that day, it seems far away, even as the darkest hour is just before the dawn.

The prophet John tells in great detail of world events that will transpire at the close of this age. Man will face some dark and difficult years when the world comes under a world government and a leader who controls men with a new money system described by John.

> And he causeth all, both small and great, rich and poor, free and bond, to receive a mark in their right hand, or in their foreheads: And that no man might buy or sell, save he that had the mark . . . or the number.   (Rev. 13:16–17)

Repeatedly, I read with amazement the statements penned by the fisherman, John. From a lonely island almost 2,000 years ago, he foretold a day when men great and small of all nations would see their old currencies suddenly canceled and replaced with a Universal Number System.

I committed the words of the prophets to memory and quoted them before audiences, civic and religious, large and small. From the Debating Hall of Oxford to the Cathedral of Calcutta; from London's Royal Albert Hall to Nairobi, capital of Kenya; I spoke through the years, not as a bigot or dogmatist with a strange doctrine, but with an honest heart. I spoke as one seeking to understand a changing world in the light of prophecy.

2

A Secret of Power

ONE STILL, cold winter night I stood high on the south bank of the Potomac, gazing across the river at the city of Washington, which sparkled in a covering of new-fallen snow.

For a third of a century, America had been the land of my adoption, and for several years Washington had been my home. To me, she was the very heart of the nation, and my own heart was part of her.

If Paris to many spelled pleasure and Rome to others represented religion, then surely Washington was a symbol of power. Was there any place in the world where her voice was not heard and her influence not felt?

Discovering America

In my early years in America, however, I had given little thought or consideration to America's place in world affairs. I was too occupied with the wonder and excitement of discovering America itself.

During a single decade, I drove over half a million miles in America, and traveled still more in the air and on the water. The sheer size of this country was staggering. I once added the territories of two dozen nations and compared their size to that of U.S.A. To my amazement, I found that the territories of

England, Ireland, Scotland, Wales, Norway, Sweden, Denmark, Holland, Germany, Switzerland, France, Belgium, Spain, Portugal, Greece, Italy, Austria, Hungary, Czechoslovakia, Poland, Romania, Cuba, Ceylon, and Japan

all combined covered less than one half of the U.S.A. In fact, one could place all of these in America twice over and still have 114,740 square miles to spare.

A Multi-Race Population

As America's population grew, so did the variety of nationalities within her borders. By the time her population reached 200 million, the races within America represented almost every land on earth.

Negroes	22,000,000
English	19,060,000
Germans	19,961,000
Irish	13,282,000
Spanish	9,230,000
Italians	7,239,000
Polish	4,021,000
Russians	2,152,000

To these, one must add the Latins, the Orientals, and others making up the balance of the nation's population.

Wealth in Few Hands

In America, one could count 100,000 men whose combined fortunes amounted to $250 billion. Some statisticians had estimated the average annual income in America at $5,000; in Latin America, $720; in Asia, $215; in China, $157. At the conclusion of World War II, the contrast between the wealth of America and the poverty of other nations stood in sharp contrast.

In 1945, Americans found themselves possessing:

70% of the free world's gold
50% of the productive power
65% of the world's telephones,
   radios, and automobiles

All of this wealth was in the hands of 6½% of the world's people, but it was not destined to remain this way for long.

Postwar Europe

At the close of World War II, I had walked in silence down the streets of London and Coventry beholding the skeletons of the buildings bombed in the blitzkriegs. In Rotterdam I gazed with awe at the endless acres of rubble. The proud Dutch city had been literally pulverized by the merciless assaults of the Luftwaffe.

With Colonel Garr I drove across France. The factories in many cities were idle. The spirit of the people seemed as shattered as their towns and villages.

In Stuttgart, I looked from the window of a bombed ruined abode, gazing incredulously at the once-beautiful city of Württemberg, now 70% in ruins.

In Berlin, I walked on what had been called the Victory Parade. I did not hear the click of the heel, nor see the Elite Guard of Hitler strutting in their proud goose step. The Victory Parade seemed lonely and empty. Berlin was 90% in ruins.

European Bankruptcy

During the many weeks we spent in Berlin, we learned firsthand some of the sorrows of war. Frau Kleist told us how she traded her treasured piano for a sack of potatoes to keep from starving and burned her furniture to keep from freezing.

In Frankfurt, Amandus Frotcher, the industrialist builder,

told how he offered his valuable rings for a quarter pound of margarine.

A Picture Reversed

In a few short years, the contrast between America's prosperity and Europe's postwar poverty vanished. Out of the war ruins of European cities, skyscrapers and modern buildings arose almost overnight.

The autobahns and expressways of Europe, once so devoid of cars, became congested with traffic; and hotels in the holiday seasons invariably hung out signs reading, "No Vacancy."

The four-word plea, "Take me to America," once familiar on almost every European's lips began to vanish.

There was no mistake. Europe along with other nations was growing richer and America poorer.

Following 1949, America's gold vanished from Fort Knox and the sub-basement of the New York City bank at the rate of $672 million a year for 10 years.

At one point in the postwar period, America had 26 billion in gold and Europeans had 10. Then the picture changed to just the reverse. Americans found themselves with approximately 10 billion and the Europeans with over 20 billion. In 1950, America owned 42% of the Free World's gold and monetary reserves. By 1971, these reserves had diminished to 8%. Millions of Americans were asking, Why? Where was America heading? What was her future?

3

The Emerging Picture

INCREASINGLY I was being invited to address audiences, civic and religious, on the subject of the New World Money System. One of the most challenging and interesting groups to which I was asked to speak was the Research Department of the United States Air Force. On December 14, 1970, I was invited to deliver a two-hour address to these men who had devoted much of their lives to science and physics.

How well I recall that bleak December evening. I could not help but contrast it with my first visit to Washington two decades earlier. Then I came in the springtime, when the cherry blossoms gave the city a beautiful dress of pink. I remembered how I had stood in the bright spring sunshine on the steps of the Capitol which cost over $24 million to erect. So quickly the calendar had brought me to 1970.

As I drove by the majestic building, I said, "You look a bit older tonight, old Capitol. You have sought to bear the burdens of a third of the world and in so doing have been unable to adequately bear your own. The men abroad who once seemed satisfied to hold your paper money became fearful that you could not redeem it, so they claimed your precious metal. Now that 60% of your gold reserves have gone, so have many of your so-called friends. But if those who have profited by your generosity predict a

10

death of the dollar, one thing is certain: their currencies will be canceled also, and the new system will affect everyone."

A New World System Predicted

Passing the Capitol, I came to the building in which I was to speak. As I studied the faces of the men assembled around the conference table, I saw that all were strangers, with one exception, Colonel Glen Balmer. Colonel Balmer was a quiet man for whom I held profound respect. His name occupied more space in America's *Who's Who* than any other man I knew.

I knew that the Colonel had a deep faith in God and also a keen interest in the subject I was to discuss. As for the other men, I presumed some would be Protestant, some Catholic, some Jewish, and others with no profession of faith at all.

I suggested in my introduction that the prophecies of the Bible could shed light on America's future and bring to light some significant truths concerning the New World Money System.

I reminded the men that in our nation, 1,665 persons suffered nervous breakdowns daily. In spite of the fact that $25 million were spent on tranquilizers and nerve medicine annually, someone was admitted to a mental institution every three minutes. According to Dr. Boggs, mental illness in America was increasing 100% faster than the population, even though science and medicine had made great progress. That very month, spokesmen for the Food and Drug Administration had suggested on national television that 70% of all American expenditures on medicine was an effort to calm the nation's ragged nerves. A recent headline had declared the economic uncertainties of the hour to be the major cause of America's nervous breakdown.

I told my audience, "I do not come as a religious bigot

seeking to force some extreme doctrine as a biased dogmatist. I will merely review the familiar facts of the day
and quote some words written by men thousands of years
ago."

I told them of John's prophecy of a day when the world
would not buy and sell with silver and gold nor any other
currency but only with a number system.

The audience of Air Force career men grew attentive and
sympathetic as I reminded them that the highly esteemed,
Robert Morris Page, inventor of pulsation radar, wrote,

> The prediction of highly significant events far in the
> future could be accomplished only through knowledge
> obtained from a realm which is not subject to the laws
> of time as we know them.

For two hours I quoted statistics and statements made by
leaders strong in faith. I concluded by quoting the utterances written by prophets of the Bible long ago and asked
the audience, in the words of Christ, "What think ye?"

At the close of my address, a strange hush came over the
entire audience. It was as though a light had penetrated a
room that shortly before had been filled with the blue patterns of cigar and cigarette smoke and the pessimism of
men.

"Yes," I said firmly, "the message of the New World
Money System is not a dark message. It is indeed very
bright. For those who understand prophecy, these are days
of amazing meaning in man's destiny."

The two hours in the conference hall had passed like so
many minutes. I received an ovation, along with a unan-
imous invitation to return.

"It is no credit to me," I told Colonel Balmer as I was
leaving. "It was really not my message. The most thrilling
part of my address had been written by men over 2,000
years ago, and I merely quoted it."

4

An Early Beginning

I SHIVERED a little from a breeze blowing up from the Potomac. "Yes, Washington," I said to the sleeping city, turning back to my car, "your sun may have set, but a bright new day is soon to dawn."

In a few minutes I was at the front door of my home at 308 Old Courthouse Road. My wife and boys had retired for the night; but burning coals on the hearth smiled cheerfully, and flickering fingers of fire beckoned to me to sit down and reminisce, and so I did.

"When did you first start speaking on the New World Money System?" I recalled Colonel Balmer asking.

"It was before World War II was fought or the United Nations, the International Monetary Fund, and the World Bank were formed," I had said. "It was before computers were invented or 'paper gold' was introduced."

"What prompted you to speak on this subject?" he asked.

The answer took me back many years.

Pulling my chair closer to the fire, I stared at the coals on the hearth. Then came a miracle that man cannot explain. Memory, with its mystical power, reconstructed in the fire the scenes of yesterday.

No, they were not merely pages from a man's diary. They were scenes of great events that pertained to all the people of the world, scenes that had continuity and order.

13

It was as though some Master mind had eliminated all of the personal incidents that had once seemed important to me in earlier life. I saw only the events that contributed to the formation of a one-world government and a new world money system.

I sat with bated breath, realizing that it was almost finished. The old currencies that had served for so many centuries would soon be canceled, and the new number system would take their place.

As I saw with clarity the scene of the final world government and the new money system, I was reminded of the paintings I had sought to place on the canvas with brush and oils. From Mombasa to the Matterhorn I had striven to capture on canvas some of the wonders of nature. I had learned that one rule in art was basic. The artist must not start with a leaf or pebble. He must close his eyes, and then open them just enough to allow a little light to fall on the object of interest. In that partial light, he first sees a horizon where the earth and sky meet. Then the profile of the mountains stand in bold relief as they touch the plains.

A 30-Year-Old Notebook

I thought of the sheafs of notes I had written on the subject of the New World Money System, and saw myself writing them through the years. On the sunny deck of the old *Queen Elizabeth,* I wrote in the mid-Atlantic. On the same ship, I wrote in the February storms while clinging to the side of the bunk or berth, striving to make the pen and paper meet, in a ship that groaned and tossed in the tempest. I saw myself writing on the veranda of a bomb-ruined hotel in Germany or in the back of an Indian warehouse in Calcutta. From Ottawa to Oxford, from Boston to Berlin, I wrote notes on the one subject that grew ever bigger and more exciting. After a time, I had a 30-year-old notebook.

My files would have been worthless to a stranger. Cards, clippings, books, and reams of paper all went into the precious collection of facts and truths. "Old fire," I said, "your friends across the world have collected most of my notes. Fires and fireplaces in a score of lands have turned most of them to ashes, and I have deigned it so. I have sought to retain, primarily, only the bold outline, the basic principles that all can understand."

My First Public Appearance

My first public utterance on the subject was in the summer of 1939, from the platform of the United Church of Canada. Dr. Robinson, the pastor, had suddenly resigned to seek a seat in the House of Parliament. The church board asked me to be the interim speaker. The black robe and high pulpit seemed a bit out of keeping with my customary surroundings, but for many weeks I spoke on.

My message on "Current Events in the Light of Bible Prophecy" was somewhat different from what the congregation had been accustomed to hearing under Dr. Robinson.

When I concluded my weeks in the church, I walked home where friends had gathered to help me make an important decision. Of course, I had only one choice—in their judgment. I was to go on to seminary to become a clergyman. Some even suggested the giving of money in an effort to persuade me to accept their well-meant advice.

"But I am not a pastor, and I never shall be," I replied. And the following Sunday found me on the platform of the theater, seeking to reach an audience that I had not reached in the sanctuary of the church. There, when I made the statement, "I may live to see the day when the world will not use silver, gold, or currencies as legal tender; but only a universal number system," Attorney Schultz winked.

My cheeks flushed with momentary embarrassment as I caught the message he conveyed to Postmaster Winram

seated across the aisle. I was embarrassed, but not angry.
My better judgment told me that the realistic attorney considered my statement too extreme to be taken seriously.
And indeed, it had been made before World War II was
declared, before nations plunged deeper into debt, before
"rationing" became a household word in the Western
world, before pollution brought its alarm signals to the
entire globe, before a world bank was formed, and before
computers were invented.

A Higher Wisdom

There was one basic difference between Attorney Schultz
and myself. He undoubtedly had filled his mind with the
recitation of the *Laws of Evidence;* and the available evidence in that hour did not seem, in his judgment, to point
toward a one-world money system, let alone a one-world
government. In contrast, my life had been filled with the
words of the prophets of the Bible. Even in that hour, I had
read and re-read the words of the prophet John, concerning
a coming world government under the control of one who,
according to John (Rev. 13:16), would cause all,

> small and great, rich and poor, free and bond, to re-
> ceive a mark . . . that no man might buy or sell, save
> he that had the mark . . . or the number.

John did not make this amazing prediction because of
his super-intelligence. He very honestly explained,

> I heard [a voice] . . . which said . . . I will shew thee
> things which must be hereafter.   (Rev. 4:1)

The prophet Daniel, like John, did not take credit for
the prophecies he uttered concerning future events. He
said,

> There is a God . . . that revealeth secrets, and maketh
> known . . . what shall be in the latter days.
>
> (Dan. 2:28)

And he added,

> This secret is not revealed to me for any wisdom that
> I have more than any living.   (Dan. 2:30)

Regarding the message of the prophets, Peter wrote,

> We have also a more sure word of prophecy; where-
> unto ye do well that ye take heed, as unto a light that
> shineth in a dark place.   (II Pet. 1:19)

A light in a dark place? This was my great reason for
declaring the message of the prophets. It was not a message of judgment written on the blackboard of destruction
with the chalk of fire and brimstone. It was a message of
hope, a message of assurance. It was the dawn of day, a
day when the sun of man's hopes would not sink into the
western skies of endless wars or a silent cemetery of the
dead. It was a light, the only light that could pierce the
war clouds of the centuries and promise man a dawn of
peace.

On the Threshold

Little did that audience realize on that quiet afternoon
in 1939 that we were already on the verge of a war that
would violently alter, almost overnight, many of the principles and patterns of life in the free world. There would
be the amassing of astronomical debt, the introduction of a
rationing system, and a hundred other factors propelling
the old world rapidly toward the formation of the new one-
world system. The prophets of the Bible, too, not only predicted a one-world system in our day, they also described

the forces that would influence its establishment; and one of the forces bringing it to pass would be the horrors of war.

Nation against Nation

The voice of King George VI trembled with emotion when on September 3, 1939, he announced the declaration of war. A strange sensation swept over me when I heard the king say,

> This war cannot be compared to any conflict in past history when army met army on the battlefield. For the first time in man's history, it is a war of nation against nation, and kingdom against kingdom.

Reaching for the Bible on my desk, I opened quickly to the passage where Christ described the events at the end of the age:

> And ye shall hear of wars and rumours of wars: see that ye be not troubled: for all these things must come to pass, but the end is not yet. For nation shall rise against nation, and kingdom against kingdom.
>
> (Matt. 24:6–7)

5

A Whole World at War

I ROSE from my chair by the fireplace to throw another log on the fire, and I said to myself, "How little do my sons, sleeping peacefully in the rooms above, know of the horrors of World War II." Over half the generation now living was not alive when World War II came to its close. Few, indeed, care to glance at the calendar of yesterday, with its vivid reminder of the awful expanse of World War II.

September 1, 1939 — Hitler invaded Poland
September 3, 1939 — Britain, Australia, New Zealand, France declared war on Germany
September 6, 1939 — South Africa declared war on Germany
September 10, 1939 — Canada declared war on Germany
April 9, 1940 — Germany invaded Norway and Denmark
May 10, 1940 — Germany invaded the Netherlands, Belgium, and Luxembourg
June 10, 1940 — Italy declared war on France and Britain
June 11, 1940 — France and Britain declared war on Italy
June 22, 1941 — Germany and Romania invaded Russia
December 7, 1941 — Britain declared war on Finland, Hungary, and Romania

19

December 7, 1941 – Japan declared war on the United States, Great Britain, Australia, New Zealand, Canada, and South Africa

December 8, 1941 – United States, France, and Great Britain declared war on Japan

December 11, 1941 – Italy and Germany declared war against the United States

December 11, 1941 – the United States declared war against Italy and Germany

December 13, 1941 – Britain declared war on the Netherlands

June 5, 1942 – United States declared war against Bulgaria, Hungary, and Romania

December 25, 1942 – Britain declared war on Thailand

October 13, 1943 – Italy declared war against Germany

July 14, 1945 – Italy declared war on Japan

August 8, 1945 – Russia declared war on Japan

The World's Greatest Armada

On June 6, 1944, my friend Colonel Al Garr crossed the channel on D-day morning. Ernest Hemingway was at his side in that assault craft. Garr, a chief ordnance officer with the First Army, described the amazing sight:

1,000 planes and gliders
2,400 U.S. and British bombers
5,049 fighter planes
3,467 heavy bombers
1,645 light and medium bombers
2,316 transport aircraft
2,591 gliders
4,000 ships
2,876,439 troops

For 60 miles, the coast of France was wet with blood of men dying on the beachheads.

Fulfilled Prophecy

In the opening hours of World War II, the king had said,

Unlike wars of the past when army met army, this, for the first time in man's history, is nation against nation and kingdom against kingdom.

The death toll of World War II bore ghastly evidence that his statement was true. In wars of the past, it was soldiers who died in greatest number, but in this war it was the civilians.

> 16,933,000 soldiers died in combat
> 34,305,000 civilians perished

Parents and children, infants and aged perished in numbers totaling twice the toll of the battlefield. While the dead paid with their lives, the living must pay with their dollars. The astronomic cost of war — both during and after — forced fathers and mothers to literally mortgage their children's future for decades.

Counting the Cost

Twenty-five years previously, the European nations had fought the First World War. In order to complete that conflict, a score of nations had come to America for economic aid.

Now, at the close of World War II, the nations once again turned to America for assistance. Were they denied? No!

America to the Rescue

On June 5, 1947, George Marshall, Secretary of State, spoke at Harvard University, outlining a plan to rebuild Europe. Congress accepted the plan and authorized $12 billion for Europe, but this was only the beginning. Eleven billion had already been given to Russia under "lend-lease."

Soon it seemed that almost every nation on earth was standing on the doorstep of Washington. None seemed to apologize for their appeals for loans or outright gifts.

Friend and foe alike went away with his requests granted, whether he was worthy or unworthy.

For my own interest I had recorded the roll call of countries who came knocking on America's door asking for aid and receiving it:

Austria	$1,170,100,000
Belgium – Luxembourg	1,935,200,000
Denmark	822,200,000
France	9,423,600,000
Germany	4,993,900,000
Berlin	127,000,000
Iceland	62,600,000
Ireland	146,200,000
Italy	5,517,000,000
Netherlands	2,416,000,000
Norway	1,024,500,000
Poland	509,400,000
Portugal	370,600,000
Spain	1,470,300,000
Sweden	108,900,000
United Kingdom	8,668,300,000
Yugoslavia	2,132,400,000
Burma	93,900,000
Cambodia	263,600,000
Republic of China	3,894,500,000
Indochina	1,535,000,000
Indonesia	558,000,000
Japan	3,462,500,000
Korea	4,486,600,000
Laos	301,200,000
Malaya	21,800,000

Philippines	1,555,700,000
Thailand	571,800,000
Vietnam	1,895,900,000
Greece	3,073,500,000
Iran	1,012,500,000
Iraq	65,300,000
Israel	709,100,000
Jordan	230,900,000
Lebanon	86,100,000
Saudi Arabia	46,600,000
Turkey	3,094,900,000
United Arab Republic	295,000,000
Yemen	11,300,000
Afghanistan	145,700,000
Ceylon	65,300,000
India	2,383,900,000
Nepal	39,400,000
Pakistan	1,255,700,000
Argentina	460,500,000
Bolivia	191,700,000
Brazil	1,376,500,000
Chile	364,600,000
Colombia	249,500,000
Costa Rica	68,700,000
Cuba	52,000,000
Dominican Republic	8,800,000
Equador	84,300,000
El Salvador	10,000,000
Guatemala	117,400,000
Haiti	80,400,000
Honduras	34,900,000
Mexico	600,000,000
Nicaragua	42,500,000
Panama	58,600,000
Paraguay	39,500,000

Peru	334,300,000
Uruguay	72,300,000
Venezuela	73,300,000
West Indies	11,500,000
Ethiopia	115,000,000
Ghana	4,000,000
Guiana	3,800,000
Liberia	73,300,000
Libya	154,000,000
Morocco	194,700,000
Nigeria	6,200,000
Somali Republic	9,100,000
Sudan	44,100,000
Tunisia	135,200,000

By 1962, America had given away over $80 billion. But the giving did not end. Soon it was 100 billion, and then 200 billion.

Too Many Creditors

Deeper and deeper America sank into debt. Prior to World War I, we prospered like no other nation on earth. Our national debt was only $2 million. Now it was so great that it would take a path of dollar bills reaching to the moon 70 times to pay it. The interest alone on the national debt was costing the American public $500 per second. Cries of "Unfair!" were increasing in volume and number from those who understood the unbelievable truth of America's bankruptcy.

By signing seven treaties, America was pledged to assist 43 countries of the world whose populations represented almost 1/3 of the world's total population.

In less than a quarter of a century following World War II, America had scattered over the world enough wealth to equal the total worth of 50 of the nation's leading cities.

$341 Billion

World War II was the most expensive war in history. It cost the United States $250 million for each day of war.

The war was declared on December 7, 1941, and continued until the Japanese surrendered on September 2, 1945. The war lasted 1,364 days. No average mind could comprehend the total cost of the war. Multiplying $250 million by 1,364 days, we see that the American people spent $341 billion as their part alone in World War II. If one sought to pay that figure at the rate of $1,000 per day, it would take almost 1,000,000 years of payments.

World War II brought suddenly and violently into the world an increased money supply, increased debts, and expanded rationing, which paved the way for the new number system. But still the cost of war was not ended. It would go on.

War Costs Continued

Peace did not end the arms race. Great nations, small nations, rich and poor, all seemed to be caught up in a mad frenzy of military spending.

In a single year, small, poverty-stricken nations that could not even feed their populations purchased the following:

        7,462 jet fighters
      141,146 armored trucks
       11,888 medium tanks
        4,693 light tanks
    2,083,087 rifles
    1,305,878 carbines
       30,878 missiles
       37,773 artillery pieces
       76,511 machine guns
        2,245 trainer planes

193 helicopters
60 destroyer escorts
35 destroyers
24 submarines
3 light-aircraft carriers

How could the smaller nations of the world continue such fearful expenditure? This shopping list of military hardware represented a financial figure greater than all the gold the world had mined from the beginning of the fifteenth century to the beginning of the twentieth century. How could money be created in such huge sums?

A spokesman in the United Nations who had studied the spiraling costs of military investments over the last decade predicted that the day was not far distant when the world would be spending $10 billion every 24 hours, if the present rate of increase continued unchecked. And strange as it seems, even with all of the attempts of peace talks and arms limitations, military investments still continue to increase.

But, I ask myself, supposing they would be limited to the present level of

$200,000,000,000 per year
or
$547,945,205 per day
or
$22,831,050 per hour
or
$380,517 per minute
or
$6,342 per second

In a day when men become calloused to crises, and insulated against emergencies, they fail to ponder the momentous affairs in which they are caught up and carried forward to the point of no return. The daily war costs of our world have reached such astronomical proportions, few indeed are capable of comprehending it. Only by illustration could one grasp in even a small measure the magnitude of man's financial problems. If a man dropped into his cash register a silver dollar every second, for a period of approximately 172 years, the total would equal the world's military expenditures for only *one* day. If ⅓ of all the poor people of the world gave their total paychecks, the amount would be insufficient to pay the yearly costs of war.

In 1867, Russia sold Alaska to the United States for $7.2 million. Thirteen years later, the Alaskan gold rush broke out, and men came from around the globe to dig gold from Alaskan soil and wash it from her rivers. After 41 years of the Alaska Gold Rush, the total yield of the precious metal was $320 million, enough to pay the present war costs of our day for only 14 hours!

In 1851, gold was discovered in Australia, the continent down under. Between 1851 and 1861, Australia produced only half a billion dollars in gold, enough to finance the modern world's military might for only one single day!

The Meaning of Money

With a hostile world daily building bigger armies, and demanding more costly weapons, how did man manufacture money in such astronomical amounts to fly the armadas of the air, and sail his ships and submarines of war? To build his bombs, and feed and clothe his armies? If he was doing this on credit, to whom was he indebted, and where and when would it all end?

To my amazement, almost no one paused to consider or ponder the meaning of money. To me, it was not a materialistic message. Money was a man's life. He earned it by the brilliance of his brain, or the sweat of his brow. Money built roads to develop lands, schools to educate children, hospitals to care for the sick. Money was bread for the children, and security for the aged. In the spiritual realm, money built churches, and gave the message of Christ to the nations of the world.

Some reflected the attitude that money was some sacred shrine which must be approached with fear and trembling, a power from a plane beyond the understanding of modern man, a system he must never question. Others took the attitude that money was a system too complicated to be understood. Early in life, I was persuaded that money was neither mystical nor·mysterious. History revealed the origin of money and its progressive use to the present hour. The prophets of the Bible foretold the ultimate end of the money system, with unmistakable detail and clarity. To understand the history of the past, and the prophecy of the future, was to have complete comprehension and understanding of the present. It was not confusing. It could be understood and explained in a layman's language.

The Power of Money

In January, 1972, I stopped on the street in Brussels and picked up a copy of the *International Herald Tribune*. In it was a quarter-page ad which had been placed by the committee promoting George McGovern for President of the United States. The caption of the ad read:

Give to the McGovern-for-President Campaign
Because You Know Money Elects the President.

Regardless of my attitude toward the candidates, I had to agree that this statement was correct. The power of money was fantastic. It had removed kings and set up kings through the centuries. It had played a part in war and peace. It could set men free, or bind them as slaves. The Bible had much to say on the theme of money. It was a drama without end. The characters who controlled money were among the most colorful on the stage of the world.

Spectacular headlines of the world's news media that shocked and startled certain people with the announcements of the coming New World Money System were no surprise to those who had watched the progressive development through the years toward a new system. In one sense, the action internationally was like a giant chess game. Much had happened even in my own lifetime. Indeed, the international manipulation of money does resemble a chess game with its kings and queens, its bishops, knights, and pawns. Early in my life, it seemed that the board was full of players, but each passing year saw the removal of the smaller men, one by one.

To me, it was exciting to watch the international moves. As the players on the board of the world became fewer, like an eager spectator, I found myself anticipating the next move in advance of its occurrence. Contemporary students of the New World Money System sometimes seem prone to place the reason for the coming system on a single factor or two. In some respects, this was an oversimplification, but I had to admit that war certainly played a major part in moving the world toward a central government and a one-world money system.

Where Does All the New Money Come From?

How well I recalled in the war years asking the important question, "How can money be created in the vast amounts necessary to carry on global wars?"

Vividly I recall one of the first war-bond rallies that I attended. The sun was shining from a cloudless California sky. The palm trees were waving in a gentle breeze that was blowing in from the Pacific. The streets of Los Angeles were crowded with people, moving in their usual leisurely pace. It was difficult indeed driving down the palm-laned avenues to appreciate the fact that men were dying on distant battlefields. As I turned down Hill Street in the heart of Los Angeles, and drove toward Pershing Square, I found myself delayed in a traffic jam. Thousands of people had filled the little park, and had overflowed into the adjoining streets. On an improvised grandstand, a band was vigorously playing martial music; flags were draped over a canopy shading the speaker from the afternoon sun. Celebrities on the platform employed the full measure of their talents, seeking to arouse the listening audience with humor, passion, and patriotism, to step up and buy war bonds. This was necessary, they said, to win the war. It was mandatory to back the nation with the buying of war bonds, when the need was for $250 million daily.

Two basic questions filled my mind. Why had the U.S. government committed the full right to print money to the Federal Reserve Bank, reserving for itself only the privilege of issuing bonds, and what was the basic difference between a bond and a dollar bill?

Edison's Opinion

Thomas Edison, the famous inventor born in Milan, Ohio, in 1847, was bitterly opposed to the policy of issuing bonds. He said,

> If our nation can issue a dollar bond, it can issue a dollar bill. The element that makes the bond good, makes the bill good also. The difference between the bond and the bill is that the bond lets the money brokers collect twice the amount of the bond.

When the government in his day wanted to borrow $30 million to develop the Muscle Shoals Project, Edison said,

> It is stupid to borrow $30 million, and have to pay moneylenders $66 million for the use of the money.

Edison was convinced that global-socialism would be brought about by the creation of debt and interest perpetrated on the nations by the international moneylenders.

Abe Lincoln Greenbacks

In 1863, Lincoln said,

> I see in the near future a crisis approaching that unnerves me, and causes me to tremble for the safety of my country; . . . money power of the country will endeavor to prolong its reign . . . until wealth is aggregated into few hands, and the republic is destroyed.

Lincoln, like Edison, felt that interest accruing on huge national debts could destroy the economy of the nation and the sovereignty of the individuals. He sought to put his good intentions into action. On February 25, 1862, he issued 150 million government dollars and then 300 million more. This $450 million of government money became known as "Abe Lincoln Greenbacks." In contrast to government bonds, they did not call for interest. Some have estimated that the money printed in Lincoln's day saved the American taxpayers over the years as much as $50 billion in interest they would have paid had Lincoln issued bonds instead of dollar bills.

Lincoln's course, however, was short-lived, for he was shot while attending the theater in Washington on April 14, 1865. Of Abraham Lincoln, Ingersoll wrote:

> Wealth could not purchase, power could not awe, this divine, this loving man. He knew no fear except the fear of doing wrong. . . . He was the embodiment of self-denial, the courage, the hope and the nobility of the nation. He raised his hands, not to strike, but in benediction.

The Power of Interest

The brilliance of Edison and the honesty of Abraham Lincoln caused each of them to speak out firmly against the dangers of national debts and compound interest. They knew that the history of the Western world for 1,694 years had forbidden the taking of usury. King Alfred the Great in 901 declared,

> If any man is found taking usury, his lands will be confiscated, and he will be banished from England.

In 1215, King John echoed the same announcement as Alfred, and as late as King James in 1566, the king declared,

> If a man is found taking usury, his lands will be confiscated. It is like taking a man's life, and it must not be tolerated.

I recalled one evening in Portland, Oregon, when I picked up a copy of the book entitled *The Chronology of Money* written by Wickliffe B. Vennard. In illustrating the power of compounded interest, Vennard suggested that if one penny had been deposited in the year A.D. 1 at 6% compounded interest, by 1895, that penny would have had an accrued value of $8,497,840 decillion! The figure so staggered my imagination, I could not comprehend it. Later that night, somewhere between midnight and dawn, I pushed back a ream of paper and concluded wearily that this man spoke the truth. For hours I had worked with pen in hand, proving to my own satisfaction that his statement was not an overstatement. Naturally, one could not comprehend the magnitude of one decillion dollars, but if it were illustrated with symbolism that could be understood, one decillion dollars would be equal to 610 quadrillion worlds of solid gold. And what would that mean? The world, I had learned in early life, weighed 6,600 billion times a billion tons.

Naturally no one would consider banking a penny with the thought of leaving it almost two millennia. But many a man could face more realistically a debt that would double in approximately 12 years, or be a thousandfold greater in a century, at the approximate rate of 6% compounded interest.

John Maynard Keynes, who wrote on the power of interest, referred to the $200,000 in gold that Sir Francis Drake gave to Queen Elizabeth, gold that he had taken from the Spanish on the high seas. This mattered little, because they had only taken it from the inhabitants of Mexico or South America. Keynes reviewed the fact that Queen Elizabeth made Francis Drake a knight for bringing home the gold, which later became part of the investment in the East India Trading Company.

"By 1930," said Keynes, *"every* dollar that Drake had brought to England would have grown in value to a hundred thousand dollars under a rate of 3¾% compounded interest."

But of what concern is this to us in our day? Lawrence R. Klein wrote in *The Keynesian Revolution* regarding national debt,

> An internally held public debt can never be a burden because we owe it to ourselves.

No burden—because we owe it to ourselves? I asked myself slowly. Is $500 per second not a burden on the taxpayers? For every tick of the clock, Americans must pay in taxes over $500 in interest on a national debt that is over $400 billion. Not a burden? Is it not a burden to pay over $1¼ billion every 30 days in taxes on interest on a national debt?

Crisis in America

With the national debt steadily increasing, the burden of interest can be counted on to raise taxes from year to year. When I moved from Canada to America in 1941, Americans were paying $31 billion in taxes. Today they must pay $336 billion. In 1942, Americans paid 23% of their individual income in taxes. By 1952, it was 29%; by 1962, 32%; and today it is 36%. This means that the average American must give all that he earns from January 1st to May 1st to pay his taxes. History shows that no economy of the past has ever survived when the taxation has reached 30% of the nation's income. History does not lie. America's economy is rapidly approaching the zero hour, the point of no return.

In 1960, T. Coleman Andrews, former head of the Bureau of Internal Revenue, said,

> I defy man or devil to contradict me when I say the dollar cannot survive another 10 years under the continued circumstances.

Andrews may have missed the time by a few years, but the fate was truthfully spoken, and he would prove to be correct.

In the same year, a series of articles was released by Bernard Baruch (once called the mastermind of Wall Street) who likened the present time to the days preceding the crash of the stock market in 1929. Young as I was at that time, I still remember some of the tragedies that followed that catastrophe.

In 1930, 1,352 banks closed their doors.
In 1931, 2,294 banks were closed.
In 1932, 31,822 businesses went bankrupt.
Between 1929 and 1932, national income fell from $83 billion to $40 billion.
Within a decade, world trade fell 57%.

As artificial fortunes vanished overnight, suicide was rampant. The clouds of depression and despair were years in clearing from the economic skies of the Western world.

Few people in America anticipated the tragic crash of '29. Reassuring voices promised the general public a smooth road and prosperity ahead. Those who were unwilling to pause and ponder the true facts were caught entirely by surprise and were emotionally unable to cope with the calamity that not only swept away their financial security, but in many cases their morale also. No, I said firmly, the dollar will not suddenly drop dead of an unexpected heart attack. Every man in the monetary world conversant with the facts of the day, has watched with mingled emotions the dollar system, like an aged friend, falling, staggering, rising again, struggling to move forward on the last lap of a journey that began centuries ago in the Middle Ages. True, its final moment may come with a measure of surprise to those who live only for the day, but the vast majority can now see the end in view and are making preparation accordingly.

Crisis in Canada

In April, 1971, I read that Horace Snifkin had said that the present science of economics was destroying the nation, and as a patriot he was resigning his prominent office in Canada and wanted no part in the disastrous future.

"Fortunately," said Snifkin, "many people do not know the true facts. They have become economically illiterate. They go along from day to day never suspecting they are already financially ruined.

"Those," he said, "who know the facts of the economy, stare at their charts in sleepless horror. We use foolish terms," he continued, "like being bankrupted into prosperity. Every true economist knows that Canada is headed for total financial disaster.

"America, too," he added, "has discarded the remedy that would cure its economic woes."

Dollar Crisis in Europe

Within a few days after I had read the statements of Horace Snifkin, I picked up a copy of the provincial newspaper, *The Albertan,* and read a headline: DOLLAR CRISIS IN EUROPE.

In three frantic hours, the West German Central Bank was forced to buy more than $1 billion in U.S. currency.

The next day, May 6, 1971, the same paper carried an Associated Press release which read,

> Several European banks have stopped buying American currency Wednesday in the face of the massive dollar-selling rush.

In August, 1971, all of Europe and the world was startled over the announcements that Europeans had closed their windows to Americans desiring to sell or exchange their U.S. dollars for European currencies. The crisis continued August 12, 13, 14, 15, 16, 17, 18. For seven long days, anger and frustration was rampant among the American tourists on the continent.

Again in March, 1973, European banks refused to accept American dollars, this time for an even longer period — seventeen days.

False Security

Often abroad I thought with sadness of the many American friends at home who felt their castle could never crumble and their securities could never be swept aside. During the summer of 1971, Europeans who had been the recipients of Amercia's generosity after the war seemed to take increasing delight in depicting her economic problems. The artists of Europe seemed to vie one with another in creating colorful covers for their magazines. *Pourquoi*

Pas showed the dollar like a ship sinking into a sea of oblivion. America's economic problems were not discussed merely by sharp-witted journalists, nor by the words of prejudiced orators. Men as famous as Dr. Klaus Noe, German economist in the Cabinet at Bonn, referred to American dollars as "printing press" money and predicted their future would be the same as that of the canceled currency of Germany in 1923.

I could not lightly brush aside the comments of Dr. Noe. For several days I had been speaking in Beethoven Hall in the capital of West Germany. The city of Bonn received us warmly, and the press covered our appearance in the city with the finest publicity we had received on the continent. Dr. Noe's words were not too different from those I had heard in Washington, D.C. My son, Robert Lee, attending his class in economics, heard the teacher say on the opening session,

> You men have come to the moment in America's history when a man might light his fire with a $10 bill as readily as with a match.

For five hours, I had sat alone with a special advisor to the U.S. President. I had been his guest in the International Board of Trade in New York, and he in turn graciously attended the meeting in which I spoke on the subject "The Death of the Dollar." Following my address, we sat together in a New York restaurant from 10:00 P.M. to 3:00 A.M. At the conclusion of our conversation, he left me with the statement,

> Your presentation, in my judgment, is flawless. The only additional comment I would add is that the situation is graver than you have depicted it.

Words seemed weak and futile to describe the emotions of one's heart when he sees his beloved America lose not only her money, but her prestige and integrity abroad. In

August, 1971, there was a sight that saddened the hearts of Americans in Paris. On the steps of the Sacred Heart Church, a poor beggar sat with hat in hand, asking for charity. Attached to the hat was a card on which the beggar had crudely scribbled four words: American Dollars Not Wanted.

If these words merely reflected an intended insult from a lone beggar, few would have cared, but the sad truth was that they all too candidly depicted the attitude of much of Europe.

No, it was not pleasant to face such scenes as this. But I would respect myself much less if I turned my eyes and mind away from the real issues of the day.

6

How Will the Dollar Die?

IF WE have come to the final days of the dollar era, it is natural to ask how money began and how it will end.

What Is Money?

Man might simply define money by saying it is, a standard of value for goods received and service rendered. Money was anything that people would accept in exchange for goods or services, in belief that they may in turn exchange it later for other goods or services.

Origin of Money

Everyone at some time or other hears interesting expressions related to money, such as "shell out" or "he paid his fee" or "not worth his salt," etc. The words "shell out" date back to the time when men used shells for money. The little cowrie or ornamental shell spread as money from China and India eastward to the islands of the Pacific Ocean and became a medium of exchange in many parts of Africa and even the Americas. Cowrie money still circulates today among the Dahomeans of the west coast of Africa. The only form of this money that ever gained international usage was this delicate pea-to-walnut size seashell that was carried around the world by the sailing traders of yesterday. In some countries, even after metal coins were introduced, the already existing cowrie shells were preferred. They were cleaner, more pleasant to handle, and impossible to counterfeit.

The expression, "paying a fee," had its origin in Germany. There the word for cattle is *Vieh,* pronounced "fee." Long ago, if a farmer wished to pay his debt to his local doctor or landlord, he would take him one of his cattle.

On occasion, we hear that someone "was not worth his salt." In India in the ninth century, salt was so scarce, it became more precious than the fabled Indian sapphires. Before the days of refrigeration, salt was used as a preserver of foodstuffs. It was placed in quills and bamboo tubes of varying lengths and sizes. About the first century A.D., salt was scarce in the Roman Empire. Mankind had not yet found a way to extract it in sufficiently large quantities from the earth or from the sea. The Roman soldiers of that time were often paid a *salarium* or "salt money." From the Latin *salarium* we receive our modern word "salary."

The Shilling

The Anglo-Saxons who invaded Britain in the sixth century came from Norway, Sweden, Denmark, and northern Germany. From 517 on through the sixth century, they moved across England from the Bristol Channel to the Irish Sea. These invaders wore metal rings and ornaments known as *schellingas*. They traded these ornaments for bread and the other necessities of life, and gradually these pieces of metal became a recognized medium of exchange. With the passing of time, the *schellingas* became the shilling of England.

The Dollar

The origin of the dollar was equally interesting. The first dollar was coined by the counts of Schlik in 1519. It was called the "Joachimsthaler," after Joachimsthal, the place in Bohemia where the silver was mined and the mint was located. The name was too long, and eventually it became shortened to "thaler." Its name changed phonetically according to the language of the country in which it was circulated. When the German Reich officially authorized the coin, it was called the "Reichsthaler." In Scandinavia, it became known as the "rigsdaler," in Holland it was the "rijksdaalder," and in Poland it was simply the "taler." Later in the eighteenth century, it became known in America as the dollar.

Money in America

When the early settlers came to America, they brought with them quite a variety of currencies from the continent. Naturally this paper money was only as good as the integrity of those who issued it. The value of that money might rise or fall in proportion to the financial strength of the institution in back of the paper currency. In olden days, communication lines were long and often interrupted. Sometimes colonists found themselves possessing paper currencies of supposed value, only to learn later that they were virtually worthless. In an effort to avoid this problem, pioneers petitioned the British government for the privilege of creating their own currency. It was denied by George III of England. Benjamin Franklin said,

> We would gladly have borne the tax on tea if we could have been granted the power to create our own money.

When the American colonists were short of money, they used almost anything as a medium of exchange. They

traded with corn and codfish and coonskins. They ex-
changed whiskey and musket-balls, tobacco and cattle. It
was all legal tender.

America's Tobacco Money

With the winning of the War of Independence, the
colonists were free to create their own money. Naturally,
there was not enough gold in their reserves to represent
sufficient backing for their paper currency. So, in states
like Virginia, Maryland, and North Carolina, tobacco was
adopted as a money standard and became a legal tender.
When plantation owners harvested their tobacco crops and
placed them in the warehouses awaiting sale, the warehouse operators issued to the owners paper receipts for
the tobacco. These receipts became transferable and were
circulated from one hand to another and even from state
to state. The tobacco receipts, indeed, became legal tender,
and in a very true sense, a form of money.

But when the price of tobacco rose and fell, the value of
the paper rose and fell accordingly. When men held paper
for any length of time, they might find the value of their
tobacco receipts greatly altered from the time when they
were first issued.

Gold

The most intriguing and by far the most universal sub-
stance used as money through the centuries is gold. In
spite of the fact that gold does not pay interest to those
who hoard it or possess it, a recent poll revealed that still
99.4% of the people of the world still crave gold. It is
beautiful to the eye. It does not rust or tarnish. In the
hands of the craftsman, it is pliable. An ounce of gold will
make a wire 50 miles long or may be pounded out in a film
so thin it can cover 100 square feet. The ancient Egyptians

knew how to hammer gold into leaves so thin that 367,000 made a pile only one inch high.

No one knows when gold was first discovered by man. At the site of Ur in Mesopotamia (now Iraq) archaeologists have discovered gold vessels made as early as 3500 B.C.

The Gold Standard

In 1870, America's banks went on the gold standard. This meant that any American could come to the bank with his paper money and exchange it for gold. In 1933, however, this was changed. In the aftermath of the crash of '29 and the depression that followed, the morale of the nation was such that it was willing to accept any revisions or suggestions which might point to a way out of their misery. Mr. Roosevelt asked the government to pass legislation demanding that the American people give up their gold. This they did, receiving in exchange paper money showing they had received $20.67 an ounce for their precious metal. Immediately, however, the government raised the price of gold to $35.00 an ounce, realizing a $3 billion profit. When asked his opinion on this particular action, Senator Carter Glass replied to President Roosevelt on April 27, 1933,

I think it is worse than anything Ali Baba's forty thieves ever perpetrated.

Elusive Gold

Thirty miles south of Louisville, Kentucky, out on the open prairie, Uncle Sam sought to prepare a storehouse for his golden billions. An army of government men blasted a mighty hole in the ground. A wall of mirrors was constructed to reflect every shadow of anything that would pass by – an airplane in the sky or a mouse crawling on the ground. Fifteen hundred soldiers stood at attention nearby, guarding night and day the steel vault containing America's gold.

And in underground vaults five stories below Wall Street reside more than a hundred thousand gold bars worth well over a billion dollars. But though this gold is on American soil, it is not ours. It bears the stamps of the central banks of any one of seventy foreign countries.

But in spite of the physical guard placed on the gold at Fort Knox and in the sub-basements of the New York banks, America's gold steadily drained away. If the gold could speak, it might impart quite a story of the miles it had traveled from country to country and from one hand to another. At the height of her power, Britain took much of the gold from the Spanish. The Spanish took it from the colonies that they invaded. At the close of World War I, when the leaders of the Western world met in the beautiful Hall of Mirrors to sign the Treaty of Versailles, Germany was compelled to deliver up all the gold she possessed in the Reich Bank of the nation. It would not be long, however, before much of America's gold would move back again to Germany and to western Europe.

In 1934, when legislation was passed prohibiting the American public from owning gold currency, the door was left wide open to the foreign holders of American dollars to claim gold in exchange for their paper. But even before this international stage was set, Representative Louis T. McFadden (R-Pa.), Chairman of the Committee on Banking and Currency, made statements on June 10 of 1932 which indicated America's gold was already moving back to Europe. His statements were recorded in the *Congressional Record* and pages 140–174 in H. S. Kenan's book entitled *The Federal Reserve Bank*. Representative McFadden speaks of those on the other side of the water with a strong banking "fence getting the currency of the

Federal Reserve Banks—exchanging that currency for gold and transmitting the gold to the foreign confederates." McFadden named the dates on which America's gold was shipped to Germany:

On April 27, 1932, $750 thousand in gold was sent to Germany. One week later another $300 thousand in gold was shipped to Germany the same way. In the middle of May of that year, $12 million in gold was shipped to Germany. . . . Almost every week there was a shipment of gold to Germany—these shipments are not made for profit.

Representative McFadden referred also to the comments of Senator Elihu Root:

Long before we wake up from our dreams of prosperity through an inflated currency, our gold which could have kept us from catastrophe will have vanished, and no rate of interest will tempt it to return.

In his report to Congress, Louis McFadden asked the question,

Why should our depositors and our government be forced to finance the munition factories of Germany and Soviet Russia?

Representative McFadden continued,

Gold was taken from the entrusting American people and was sent to Europe. In the last several months $1,300,000,000 in gold has been sent to Europe— every dollar of that gold once belonged to the people of United States and was unlawfully taken from them.

As I weighed the words of Louis McFadden and other lawmakers, I also witnessed the fantastic scene of America's vanishing gold. The record was unbelievable:

1949 — $24,500,000,000
1958 — $21,593,000,000
1959 — $20,478,483,000
1960 — $19,420,997,000
1961 — $17,667,587,000
1962 — $15,997,647,000
1965 — $13,733,000,000

On and on the gold drain went, unabated. Then came the crisis in the spring of 1968. We were living in Europe at that particular time. On March 14, hysterical crowds of people crowded, screamed, and scrambled their ways to the windows of the banks of England, and to the bank windows of the sub-basements of Paris to exchange their paper for gold. On one single day, the crude and the cultured, the peer and the peasant, carried off 200 tons of the precious metal. They stored it in secret places of their homes and deposited it in various banks in strongboxes labeled with fictitious names.

On that day Senator Everett Dirksen in conversation with Secretary of the Treasury Fowler, William McChesney Martin, and a dozen other senators said,

We have reached the bottom of the barrel.

It seemed like only yesterday when I spoke on monetary matters when America had $26 billion in gold in her treasuries. By June 30 of 1971, it had been reduced to $10.5 billion.

Inflation

Why did the people of Europe and Britain crowd hysterically into their banks on March 14, 1968, to exchange $240 million in paper for 200 tons of gold? They could not eat their gold for food. They could not wear it for clothes. It was too heavy to carry on the streets as a legal tender or medium of exchange. Why did they prefer to have the precious metal in place of their paper money?

The answer was extremely clear. They were afraid that their paper would be canceled with the stroke of a legislative pen. It would be as worthless as the German marks of 1923 when it took a wheelbarrow load to buy a simple sandwich or hot dog. The average man knew his paper money was becoming of less and less value. Americans could recall 1937 when $30 a month would put food on the table for a family of four. By 1947, the same food would cost $43. By 1957, it would cost $72. Then $100, and inflation continued unchecked.

The British, too, looked at their paper with its diminishing value. The record was indeed far from encouraging. The monetary facts offered little hope for the survival of their paper. In 1930, the official value of the pound was $4.86. In 1952, $2.82; in 1967, $2.40.

In May of 1973 on the streets of Tokyo, I stared with incredulity at the spectre of inflation in Japan. Ground beef that was selling in October for $1.40 per pound was now $2.87; orange juice was over $3.00 per glass; steak, $16.00 per pound. In less than a year the price of real estate had doubled, and wool had tripled. Hashimoto, Secretary General of the ruling Liberal Democratic Party tried in vain to reason with the financial giants of his country. He concluded that those in a position to affect the inflation were too strong and beyond control.

The problem of inflation was worldwide. Since World War II, the currencies of over 100 nations had been devalued, some many times. I recalled a 1959 address by Robert Anderson, Secretary of the Treasury. He bluntly spelled out the technique of inflation:

Suppose tomorrow morning I want to write a check for $100 million, and the treasury does not have the money. I call the Federal Reserve Bank and ask, "Will you loan us $100 million at 3½% for six months if I send you over our note to that effect?" The officer of the Federal Reserve Bank would naturally say, "I will." He would merely create that much money subject to Reserve requirements by crediting our account in the sum and accepting the government note as an asset. When I finished writing checks for $100 million, we would have added 100 million to the nation's money supply. This, he added, is one of the principles by which the 1940 dollar has shrunken to 41¢ with a quadrupling of our money supply.

Nations continuing programs of war and welfare and other costly programs, were forced to continue borrowing money. America increased her federal budget 84% in a five-year period. By going deeper in debt, she also increased her money supply 47%. Consequently, the buying power of the dollar continued to fall ever lower. In certain countries of the world, it was overwhelming. In Argentina, inflation increased 289% in a five-year period. In Brazil, over 500%. In Java, 1,000%. As the cry of inflation was heard around the world and received with genuine alarm, governmental leaders strove in vain to curb this economic disease that would spell death to all systems eventually. In September 29, 1972, the Dallas *Times Herald* showed that in that particular year inflation had increased

> Japan — 7.5%
> Great Britain — 12.5%
> France — 5.7%
> West Germany — 6.0%

Ludwig Erhard, Germany's Minister of Finance at the close of World War II, had said,

Give us depression or problems, but not inflation, for it spells eventually certain death to any economy.

Erhard knew that inflation, allowed to continue, was like sending a pilot across the ocean with a plane in which was insufficient fuel. There came unavoidably a point of no return when the pilot found he had insufficient fuel to take him to either shore.

Too Much or Not Enough

In spite of the fact that the U.S. government had increased its money supply 47% in a five-year period, and other nations were doing the same thing, still there were those who cried it was not enough. Between 1954 and 1965, world trade had doubled. I sat with a thousand delegates in the International Board of Trade in the Waldorf Astoria Hotel of New York listening to the speakers struggle with their unsolved problems. World trade had reached the staggering figure of $159.2 billion. The currencies and credits with which they had to carry on this volume of trade was little more than $67.3 billion. By 1973, the volume of trade in the free world was $367 billion. I talked with Mitchell Sharpe, then Minister of Finance for Canada, and some of the American leaders. These men realized that the currencies being used were outmoded and insufficient for the modern day. They pointed out that the system was medieval, serving acceptably in the olden days when communities were small and self-contained, but thoroughly inadequate for the present. The leaders of the nations involved in trade spoke of the nightmarish task of trying daily to adjust the varying exchange rates between the currencies from country to country on a day-to-day basis. They clamored for a single system of standardized value large enough in volume to allow world trade to move forward in an orderly fashion.

In 1967, two years following that International Board of Trade meeting in New York, the world leaders met in Rio. In discussing the inadequacy of the present world money systems to carry on world trade, Guido Carli from Rome suggested ersatz money which would resemble paper gold which was to be presented to the world the following year. I was back in America when the announcement came. It was March 31, 1968. Most of the world reacted with amazement at the announcement that came from Europe stating that the nations of the world were ready to transact business with a new medium of exchange known as "paper gold." But to all who follow the trend of monetary matters, the announcement was no surprise. For days there was a feeling in the air that something momentous was coming. An editor wrote in the *Financial Times,*

Something sinister is going on.

With great interest, I followed the comments and reactions of world leaders.

Carl Schiller, Germany's financier, stated,

There's a worm in the apple somewhere.

Pierre Paul Schweitzer seemed pleased. Schweitzer, the nephew of Albert Schweitzer, was an elite Protestant, born in Alsace-Lorraine, who had served as number-three man in the Bank of France, and had been elected managing director of the International Monetary Fund. Some declared that when paper gold was presented to the world on that March morning, Schweitzer declared,

Gentlemen, we are right on schedule.

72% of the nations in the IMF were considered under-developed. Schweitzer seemed especially dedicated to the task or policy of taking from the rich to give to the poor. This naturally made him popular with the majority in the IMF, who were elated at the prospect of acquiring some of America's wealth regardless of the measures.

Why the Announcement from Europe?

Many Americans, startled by the announcement of paper gold, were asking, "Why has this declaration come to us from the bankers of Europe? Why did we have to hear it first from the lips of the spokesmen representing the gold pool so integrated with the World Bank and the International Monetary Fund?"

The attitude of the average man on the street was one of absolute helplessness. In olden days, banking had been a rather personal matter between himself and a trusted friend. It had changed with the passing of time until it was with an institution equally trusted and respected. The local banker was indeed his friend and would discuss with sincerity the personal financial needs of any of his clients. But banking had become much more than a localized or even nationalized institution. In a single lifetime it had seemingly taken on an ominous new form of world control.

A question began to arise in the hearts of millions of Americans. "Why can't we retain our financial destiny in our own hands? Why can't banking be a personal matter between man and his banker as in the past? Why must it be in the international courts and the arenas of the world?"

In searching for the answers to those questions, I seemed to find a twofold answer. Logic and wisdom could explain with clarity the reasons for a world bank. But there was a dark side, which, when properly considered, revealed an invisible government with an amazing power that planned world control in a sinister fashion.

7

Banks and Bankers — Yesterday and Today

The Origin of Banking

Banking may have been born in Babylon 3,000 years ago. The first banking transactions may well have been carried on by two men. A possessor of gold might find it undesirable to carry the heavy metal with him on a journey. If unable to carry his treasure conveniently, he found it most desirable to leave it in the custody of a trusted friend. The custodian of the gold would stamp his signet on a piece of parchment or leather which represented a receipt for the precious metal. At a later date, anyone presenting this receipt to the guardian of the gold could retrieve the treasure. This system in the beginning was as simple as the present-day policy of leaving one's car on the parking lot and retrieving it by presenting the ticket to the parking lot attendant.

As the system grew more popular, qualified personalities found themselves guarding the gold for numerous men who trusted them with their treasures.

Fractional Moneylending

With the passing of time, these owners of gold traded their receipts between each other in business transactions.

52

But seldom did they come to collect in bags the heavy metal which was impractical to carry from place to place. After much experience, the guardians of gold were able to ascertain the percentage of gold that would actually be collected by the owners under normal circumstances. Although the precious metal did not belong to them (it was still the property of those who had entrusted it to their care), these guardians of gold began to lend the precious metal to others who were willing to pay a percentage, called "usury," for the use of it. It was not long until these guardians of gold became known as "lenders" as well as guardians. And because they would lend as much as 80% of the gold they were guarding, they became known as "fractional moneylenders." Like most programs developed by man, the system could prove to be of great worth and benefit if properly used, but it could also be a monster of evil if abused.

Banks in America

Our founding fathers and early Colonists faced an impossible situation in monetary matters.

As banks sprang up in the New World and issued their own paper money, they operated under state laws and licenses granted them by their local state government. Confusion began to reign as people moved from state to state carrying various forms of paper of diverse value.

The National Bank Act

In 1863, Abraham Lincoln influenced the passing of the National Bank Act. This provided for a system of private banks that would receive their charters only from the government and operate on a given standard of values and regulations.

The Federal Reserve Bank

On December 23, 1913, Woodrow Wilson influenced legislation which established the Federal Reserve Bank or the Federal Reserve System. With the establishment of the Federal Reserve System, the United States government forfeited the right to create its own money. The government retained the power only of issuing government bonds upon which the taxpayers paid interest to the Federal Reserve System which alone had the power to issue the currency known as Federal Reserve Notes. The attitude of government men toward the Federal Reserve System was interesting, to say the least. Some lauded its virtues, and others deplored its dangers. Some referred to the Federal Reserve System as "the banks' bank" and declared it was necessary to safeguard the local bankers in times of crisis.

Financial Crisis, June 19–23, 1970

On June 19, 1970, the American people escaped a national economic crisis by a mere hairline. The sixth largest enterprise in the United States, the largest railroad of the country, the Pennsylvania Central,. went bankrupt. The bankers were confident that the government would bail them out. They gathered in the northwest conference room of the tenth floor of the Federal Reserve Bank of New York to sign the papers as soon as the word came from Washington.

But Congressional disapproval had been hardening. Wright Patman, chairman of the House Banking Committee, refused to grant the $200 million loan, declaring it would be "only the beginning of a welfare program for the giant corporation." What could be done? The Federal Reserve System had been criticized for cutting off money too abruptly in 1966 and of increasing it too fast in 1967 and early 1968.

If stockholders across the nation became concerned that their stocks in this or any other company were to lose their value, they could commence a run on banks in seeking to cash in their stocks that would deplete the reserves of the banks of America and throw the entire nation into chaos. Needless to say, tension was high, and furious action was taken to stave off a national panic that could have created havoc in those days between June 19 and 23. Bankers of the nation lined up for loans of $1.7 billion hoping to be able to meet the demands for money that would be brought to them by fearful stockholders wishing to exchange their paper stock for money.

Too few Americans realize that the banks of the nation operate much the same as the "Fractional Money Lenders" of the past. If a large number of people were to desire their money from the bank at one time, the banks would have only a fraction of the amount needed. A national scare like the collapse of the Pennsylvania Central Railroad could have started such a situation. This is why private banks strove to borrow extra money from the Federal Reserve in the face of such an impending crisis.

The World Bank

In 1944 a World Bank was born, an infant that soon grew into a mighty giant. The national problems that had brought into existence a National Banking Act and the Federal Reserve System were identical in many respects to the problems that brought about the establishment of the World Bank. In the early pioneer days, men could do business with a local bank because few traveled far from home and seldom crossed the borders of another state. Even by the turn of the century, few men had traveled more than three hundred miles.

Overnight, the entire scene changed. With the age of automation, world travel became common. Men traveled across the oceans as easily as across the street. In a single year,

> 108 million Americans
> took 360 million trips
> totaling 312 billion miles.

International Monetary Fund

In Europe, I watched the frustrations of people moving from one country to another carrying in their pockets a variety of currencies, each with a different value and a changing exchange rate from day to day. From the Bon Marché of Brussels to the American Express Office of Frankfurt or the Hilton Hotel of Rome, I have heard angry voices at the cashier's window declaring their currency to be worth more than the exchange rate they were being quoted.

If the inconveniences and the frustrations of the individual were obvious, the merchants of the world were a thousand times more agitated. They dealt in multi-million dollar transactions. If they bought or sold on a given day when the exchange rate was at one figure, only to find days or hours later the exchange rate had varied, they might face either exorbitant profit or total bankruptcy.

They cried for an International Monetary Fund that would guarantee stabilization and protect them against the daily fluctuations on a violent scale. Just as the local pioneers wanted their local banks to be governed by a national banking act, now various nations of the world were asking for some form of international control. They turned their eyes to the United Nations and to the agency that had been established within the UN called the International Monetary Fund.

The International Monetary Fund was established in 1944 at the Bretton Woods Conference in the United States.

At the outset, it was viewed with suspicion by some of the countries reluctant to forego their national sovereignty. At first the membership was only 27 nations, then it grew to 45, finally to 100, and on to 124. Certain rules were laid down and nations were expected to follow them.

The Fund, for example, refused to lend to countries that would alter their exchange rates by more than 10% without the approval of the International Monetary Fund. With the formation of the IMF, other names began to appear prominently in the world arena, names such as the World Bank, the G-10 (standing for Great Ten), and the Gold Pool. It was a spokesman from the latter, on March 31, 1968, who introduced "paper gold."

"Paper gold" — the name was indeed intriguing, but it was a misnomer. It was neither paper nor gold but only a number placed by the name of the nation. The amount of that number was called a "drawing right" and was abbreviated with three initials "SDR" standing for "Special Drawing Right." With the announcement of paper gold, and the proposal that some $10.5 billion of it be issued in the first sixty-month period, the spokesman for the world body emphasized it was only for international use. Behind the closed doors of the conference room, however, other world leaders reputedly said it would be the system in the near future for every individual on earth.

Only 12 months and 17 days prior to the announcement of paper gold, I was flying into Denver, Colorado. I was scarcely conscious of the plane touching the runway, for I found myself engrossed in an article in the February 14, 1967, issue of the *U.S. News & World Report*. The article was written by George Mitchell of the Federal Reserve System. It pictured a telephone in every home attached to a computer that carried the owner's name or number. The phone was not installed for social or business reasons. It was merely a connecting line to the computer or the data center which carried the home owner's number, and also his drawing right. When a personal need arose for himself or for his family, the owner would pick up the phone and learn from the computer at the other end what he could or could not have. This was called his special drawing right. So the system introduced on March 31, 1968, would indeed expand until it became universal and all-inclusive. As I pondered the fearful possibility of the financial control of men and nations in the hands of an international committee, I found myself remembering again the words of Meyer Amschel Rothschild:

> Give me control over a nation's economy and I care not who writes its laws.

And the words of Lord Gladstone:

> The government . . . in the matters of finance must leave the money power supreme and unquestioned.

And the words of Chancellor Reginald McKenna:

> They who control the credit of a nation direct the policy of the governments and hold in the hollow of their hand the destiny of the people.

And Karl Marx, who said in his *Manifesto,*

> Money plays the largest part in determining the course of history.

Who Will Control the Money?

Communist or capitalist, banker or president of the nation, all men seemed to agree that those who controlled the finance of a nation represented a power greater than any other legislative body.

I recalled an afternoon in Brussels when I addressed an international group in the Metropole Hotel. Apart from

John Bains of the *Brussels-Phoenix Press,* the audience were strangers to me. Most of the men present held high office in various departments and were favorably disposed toward the new system on which I was to speak. I concluded my luncheon address by saying, "Gentlemen, you look with approval upon this coming new order and the new system it will bring. You believe it has the answers to some of the frustrations and unanswered problems of the present moment, but I, in all sincerity, would like to ask you one basic question before leaving you today: who will control it?"

A hush fell over the room. I looked from face to face in search of an answer. On one side sat a four-star general, on the other, an attorney. None offered to speak.

"Perhaps," I said, "you feel that none of us has the answer to this question: Who will hold in his hand your future in this new international government with its new world money system? But there is an answer. It is spelled out clearly by a man who lived 2,000 years ago and described these very days."

Opening my Bible, I read once again the familiar words of John, the prophet, who wrote concerning a world government and its leader who would hold power

over all kindreds, and tongues, and nations . . . and causeth all, both small and great, rich and poor, free and bond, to receive a mark in their right hand, or in their foreheads: And that no man might buy or sell, save he that had that mark . . . or the number.

(Rev. 13:7, 16–17)

The Invisible Government

On March 22, 1922, John F. Hylan, mayor of New York City, made the following statement:

The real menace of our republic is the invisible government which, like a giant octopus, sprawls its slimy length over our city, state, and nation. At the head is a small group of banking houses, generally referred to as "international bankers."

To what extent did international bankers exercise ownership or control over America's Federal Reserve System?

The public in general assumed that the stock in the Federal Reserve System was owned by America's private banks, but apparently this was not voting stock. For years I observed those who were genuinely concerned over this very grave question. The men concerned were often the most astute business men and lawmakers of our land, some as prominent as Wright Patman, Chairman of Banking and Currency. In 1941 Congressman Patman wrote concerning this question to Marriner S. Eccles, Chairman of the Board of Governors for the Federal Reserve Bank. On April 18th of that same year Congressman Patman received a reply from Eccles which read,

> This so-called stock ownership, however, is more in the nature of enforced subscription to the capital of the Federal Reserve Bank than an ownership in the usual sense.

More than a quarter of a century later, Mr. Patman was still trying to get an answer, from the chairman of the Board of Governors of the Federal Reserve, then William McChesney Martin:

> The stock, or that word "stock" is a misnomer, is it not?

Mr. Martin's answer:

> If you were talking about stock in terms of proprietorship ownership — yes.

Mr. Patman continued,

Then the word "stock" is a misnomer. It is not correct at all. It is just an involuntary assessment that has been made on the banks as long as they are members. Therefore, the statement that the banks own the Federal Reserve System is not a correct statement, is it?

Mr. Martin:

The banks do not own the Federal Reserve System.

As I pondered the words of Wright Patman and the statements of many other prominent lawmakers on Capitol Hill through the years, it seemed that a great number of prominent senators and congressmen had expressed their concern that the financial power of America was held not in the hands of its local bankers or its lawmakers, but rather in the hands of a few international bankers who exercise their control over not only America but also western Europe.

Is there, in truth, a small group of international bankers controlling the world's financial destiny, even as Mayor Hylan of New York declared?

Paul Warburg

Who *was* responsible for the formation of the Federal Reserve? None other than the scion of Hamburg's famed banking House of Warburg—Paul Warburg. Regarding Mr. Warburg, Professor E. R. A. Seligman, himself of the international banking family and head of the Department of Economics at Columbia University, said,

The Federal Reserve Act is the work of Mr. Warburg more than of any other man.

The Honorable Louis McFadden, Chairman of Banking and Currency Committee, seemed to reach the same conclusion. On March 4, 1933, he said to Congress,

We know from assertions made here by the Honorable John Garner, Vice-President of United States, Paul Warburg did come here from Hamburg, Germany, for one purpose — to take over the treasury of United States as the international bankers have done with the treasuries of Europe.

Regarding the so-called group of international bankers, Mr. McFadden said further on June 10, 1932,

It controls everything here, and it controls all our foreign relations. It makes and breaks governments at will.

Paul Warburg had a son named James P. Warburg. On February 17, 1950, he stood before the U.S. Senate and declared,

We shall have world government whether or not we like it. The only question is, whether world government will be achieved by conquest or consent.

The House of Rothschild

Meyer Amschel Rothschild (1743–1812) of Frankfurt, Germany, studied originally to be a rabbi. Later, however, he turned his interests to finance and, with his five sons, established the famous banking house in Frankfurt. Four of the sons were later sent to Vienna, London, Paris, and Naples to set up branches of their family bank. This combine soon became the most powerful banking establishment of Europe. Amschel Rothschild, the eldest son, remained with his father in Frankfurt and became the treasurer of the German Confederation. Salomon, the second son, founder of the Vienna branch, became a leading personality in the Austro-Hungarian Empire. Nathan, the third son, founder of the London branch, became the most powerful man in English finance. Carl, the fourth son, founder of the Naples branch, became one of the most powerful men in Italy. James (Jacob), the fifth son, founder of the Paris branch, soon dominated the financial destiny of France. By 1850, the House of Rothschild represented more wealth than all the royal families of Europe and Britain combined.

International Bankers

The House of Warburg, the House of Rothschild, the few other powerful banking houses became known as "the international bankers." They are described best by Dr. Carroll Quigley who taught at Princeton and Harvard. He did research in the archives of France, Italy, and England and authored several widely read books. When Dr. Quigley decided to write *Tragedy and Hope* (Macmillan, 1966), he knew he would be exposing one of the best-kept secrets in the world. Regarding the international bankers, Dr. Quigley states,

> They remained different from ordinary bankers in distinctive ways: (1) they were cosmopolitan and international; (2) they were close to governments and were particularly concerned with questions of government debts; (3) their interests were almost exclusively in bonds and very rarely in goods; (4) they were, accordingly, fanatical devotees of inflation; (5) they were almost equally devoted to secrecy and the secret use of financial influence in political life. These bankers came to be called the international bankers.

In quoting Dr. Quigley, W. Cleon Skousen comments on page 4 of his book entitled *The Naked Capitalist,*

> Dr. Quigley makes it clear throughout his book that, by and large, he warmly supports the goals and the purposes of the network. If that be the case, why

should he want to expose a world-wide conspiracy and disclose many of its most secret operations? Obviously disclosing the existence of a mammoth power network which is trying to take over the world could not help but arouse the vigorous resistance of the people who are its intended victims, so why did Dr. Quigley write this book?

Quigley's answer appears in a number of places, but it is especially forceful and clear on pages 979–980. He says, in effect, that now it is too late for the little people to turn back the tide. In a spirit of kindness, he is therefore urging them not to fight a power that is already established. All through his book, Dr. Quigley assures us that we can trust these benevolent well-meaning men who are secretly operating behind the scenes. They, he declares, are the hope of the world. All who resist them represent tragedy, hence the title of his book. Dr. Quigley states,

I know of the operations of this network because I have studied it for twenty years, and was permitted for two years in the early 1960's to examine its papers and its secret records. I have no aversion to it, nor to most of its aims, and have for much of my life been close to it, and to many of its instruments.

According to W. Cleon Skousen,

Dr. Quigley expresses the utmost contempt for members of the American middle class, who think they can preserve what he calls their "petty bourgeois" property rights and constitutional privileges.

After pondering these writings, I asked myself how far back one could trace this organized plan for control of world finance. On July 4, 1856, Benjamin Disraeli declared before the British House of Commons,

The world is governed by very different personages from what is imagined by those who are not behind the scenes.

Some of the strongest words that came to my attention were those of Curtis B. Dall, written in Philadelphia, Pennsylvania, on April 1968, as an introduction to H. S. Kenan's book on the Federal Reserve Bank. In reference to the international bankers, Mr. Dall writes,

They are driving toward complete control of the world's long-range monetary policy and principal world markets for their own profit. They foment foreign wars to aid this objective.

It did not take a brilliant mathematician long to prove with simple arithmetic that war debts allowed to continue would soon burden the people of the world with such indebtedness that it would take most of the earning power of the masses simply to pay the compounding interest. Was it possible, I asked myself repeatedly, that men could so crave power that they would be willing to sacrifice millions of lives to the god of war in order to achieve their goals? If it were true, were they so deluded or deceived that they justified the mass slaughter of the innocent as a so-called stepping-stone to a better world they were seeking to build? Regardless of the questions, or their answers, there was one certain fact: the world was swiftly moving toward centralized government and universal control. The General Assembly of the United Nations frequently echoed with accusations and dissension. But there was one power that seemed even stronger than man's endless legislation. It was the power of money. Whoever controlled it, controlled man's destiny. The path toward world control seemed to be indeed a divided highway. On one side, there were the shadowy personalities representing the high priests of finance, who visualized the wealth of the world in few hands – their hands. On the other side of the road, there were a number of men, honest and sincere, who pointed out that the total commitment to a world government was man's only hope of escaping a nuclear holocaust. Or famine from exploding population, or poison from pollution.

Checks Obsolete

Members of the Federal Reserve warned that the nations' banks could strangle on the 22 billion checks the Americans wrote each year, pointing out that in a hundred months the number of checks would double. They urged the adoption of a computer system which would automatically transfer funds between bank accounts. A person's pay would automatically be credited to his bank account by his employer, without the writing of a check. And the regular payments which the worker owed – car payments, rent, etc. – would automatically be sent to his creditors' accounts when due. George Mitchell of the Federal Reserve declared it was most urgent to reform the checking system before the economy smothered under a pile of paper.

I did not know George Mitchell personally, but I did know many honest and sincere bankers who shared his sentiments. There was Carlos Verheek of the Kredietbank of Belgium, and Banker Keller of Germany.

Mountains of Paper

As I sat with Banker Keller in his Stuttgart office, I heard him heave a weary sigh. "We are being buried under paper," he said sadly. From the doorway of his office I could see the lines of people standing impatiently before the bank tellers.

I knew that back home our government was spending $350,000 a minute. The welfare program alone was costing the taxpayers more than a billion dollars a month. In a four-year period, the federal budget had increased 84% and in five years the money supply 47%.

In America, I had talked with my banker friends. Without exception, every banker realized we were coming to the end of an old regime and the dawn of a new era. Our early ancestors had used shells, iron, cotton, or cattle as a medium of exchange. Then gold. Now, the paper currencies were becoming as antiquated as all of the obsolete systems that man had used. A new system was about to dawn over the western world and it would be a number system, made possible by the birth of the computer in 1946.

8

The Computer Age

WHAT fantastic progress computer technology has made in the last quarter century! On February 15, 1971, I pondered the words spoken by Dr. Brainard, as he described the first computer at Penns Morre School of Engineering. It weighed 30 tons, and occupied 1,500 square feet of space. Today, infinitely more complicated computations are done by common garden-variety computers, occupying no more office space than a junior executive.

Computers that could register one character per second had been made obsolete by those that could register a thousand characters per second (or one character per millisecond). The progression went from milliseconds to microseconds to nanoseconds. When computers reached the place of registering in nanoseconds, or one billion characters per second, I said, Surely this is the ultimate. Nothing in this world will ever exceed that speed of computation.

But by New Year's Day of 1973, IBM technicians were speaking of picoseconds, which would mean the computer would register one trillion characters per second.

For the Nation and the World

A virtual network of computers began to be tied together in unity over the nation. Large computers drove small ones, which in turn drove a multitude of terminal units which would be placed in every home and place of business.

Connected with Telstar, a man could be in any country or island of the sea where a mechanical device was within reach of his hand and by registering his own number on the mechanical device, he could send a message to Telstar and on to his local bank, and receive it back again in his corner of the world—all in ten seconds of time. Surely the stage was set for the marvelous and mysterious operation of a universal number system.

TRW Credit Data was adding 50,000 names a week to its data center, and claimed they would soon have a complete record of everyone who had ever used credit.

Increased Concern

Along with the wonders of the developing system, more and more people became alarmed that they were being homogenized into a maze of wheels and tapes. This concern was not the expression of the emotional or the illiterate; qualified speakers spoke openly, and brilliant writers wrote freely on the dangers of being swallowed up in a great machine. Senator Ed V. Long of Missouri said,

> I must report to you that the right to privacy is being dangerously and recklessly ignored and violated.

Dr. Orville G. Brim, Jr., head of the Russell Sage Foundation, said,

> There is no doubt that we can run the society better with this information but doing this could well be in conflict with all our fears of having privacy invaded.

Every American's Record on One Roll of Tape

I recalled the day that NASA gave the contract to Honeywell for the production of the laser computer. It was

reported that this computer could document on a single roll
of tape all of the vital statistics of every American in the
nation. The claim was also made that this marvelous machine had instant playback.

This would mean that a stranger from Savannah, Georgia,
could walk into an office in San Diego, or Seattle, and give
them his number. Before he could cross the street, the office
would have all the vital statistics concerning that stranger.
His place of birth, his education, his training, his profession, his criminal record, his health record, and his religious inclinations.

A Machine with No Heart

While pondering the power of the computer age, I recalled a moment in a travel agency on Lake Street in
Pasadena, California. I stepped to the counter on a beautiful June afternoon to pick up my air tickets. On leaving the
building, I heard the troubled voice of a little mother,
which caused me to pause and listen to her problem.

"I am sorry, ma'am," said the airline officer, "but you
have no tickets."

"But I made my reservations over two weeks ago. Only
yesterday I phoned in to reconfirm the fact you were holding my reservations for me."

"I'm sorry," replied the clerk again, "but you have no
tickets on this particular flight, and no space is available."

I watched the mother's face cloud with anxiety, and the
children by her side blinked to hold back their tears. It was
the beginning of the holiday season, the rush had already
begun, and all flights going from Los Angeles to Atlanta
that day were fully booked.

"It was so important that we leave this evening," said the
little mother in great distress. "Please, is there no one I
can talk to personally?"

Then came an answer that rang in my ears for many days, an answer I would never forget.

The clerk looked blankly into the face of the troubled customer, and replied, "Ma'am, the computer apparently canceled your reservations, and no one talks back to the computer."

I turned down the street saying to myself that the new era is both fantastic and fearful. Men have created a machine that has almost supernatural brains but no heart at all.

One Card—One Number

When I arrived at our home back in Washington, D.C., in the summer of 1968, my telephone rang. I answered the call, and a stranger in New York introduced himself as Mr. White, and said he would like to ask me some questions. He asked my place of birth, and also regarding my employment, how long I had been engaged in my particular profession.

The speaker had a congenial voice and chatted as leisurely as though he were in my living room. I watched the minutes tick off on the clock. I knew that he was calling long-distance and every minute was costing money.

With a warm, reassuring voice, the party from New York answered my eventual queries, "No, sir, we are just updating our credit files."

"Yes, your credit record is perfect, but we feel we must keep in step with the times."

When the phone conversation finally concluded, I turned the plastic pockets of my wallet. There was the Diners Club card, the Carte Blanche, the American Express, the Bank of America, the Master Charge, the telephone card, the Standard Oil, Texaco, Shell Oil, and Gulf Oil cards, the Sheraton Hotel card, and the Ambassador TWA card. Laughingly, I said to myself, "My wallet is almost too heavy to carry and contains everything but money." Every card represented a number, and I could easily understand why the move was on to consolidate all of these into a single number. Even as I thought about the significance of the computer system, I realized the government was spending $2 billion every twelve months in operating 2,500 computers that soon would have complete mastery of man's privacy and control of his every action. In spite of the well-grounded fears of millions of people, the number system had dawned and would dominate their immediate future.

It seemed indeed to make a lot of sense to consolidate all of man's cards and numbers into one. Men who discussed the number system went beyond the suggestion of a single card. They declared this, too, could be lost or stolen.

Almost daily we began to hear suggestions that each man be given a lifetime number that could be permanently impressed on his flesh. In Europe I had heard the spokesman on the Frankfurt radio station discussing the idea of tattooing man's number on the face. When placed on the flesh, they said, a number could not be lost, nor could it be stolen from the owner.

In America, I talked with a friend who was with the Northwest National Bank. He spoke of the progress being made in the laboratories in developing an invisible, nontoxic ink which would be tattooed on man's flesh, invisible in normal light, but clearly legible in a special light.

One of my friends in the news media said even the president pointed out the value of such a system. If man merely had a number, it would not only reduce to almost zero the causes for crime on the street, but would also prove to be a deterrent to major crimes such as plane hijacking. Why vould a man try to rob a man or bank or hijack a plane if all he could collect would be a number?

Imagine, life without money . . . No more checkbooks to balance, no more debts to re-finance (presumably the computer would automatically stop our credit if we were about to exceed our earning capacity), no more worries about inflation or devaluation. What freedom, what bliss!

There was only one small prerequisite: for such a system to work, it would require every man to have a number. Were a man to refuse to wear his number, there would be no way to incorporate him into the system.

As the prophet had predicted almost two thousand years previously,

No man might buy or sell, save he that had . . . the number.

9

Coming to the End

IN THE SPRING of 1939, two things seemed extremely secure: the dignity of the individual and the sovereignty of his money. Almost overnight, however, everything changed. With the declaration of war, man's own interests were ignored. The interest of the nation came first, and rules and regulations were not made in the interest of individuals; they were made in the interest of the nation's survival.

Raw materials and manufactured goods were being channeled into war usage. Domestic demands ran much higher than supply. Rationing was immediately established. Men were issued little books of paper coupons on which were printed numbers.

I watched the power of this system in effect in almost every walk of life, and in several lands.

Rationing in Britain was extremely severe. For thirteen years, the British knew the miseries of rationing. During the most extreme years, the Englishmen received one egg per week, and two ounces of beef per week, per person. Bad as his plight was, the last days of the war and the immediate postwar years were even worse for the Germans. Amandus Frotcher in Frankfurt told me of cases in Germany where men were shot to death for the crime of possessing a pig.

74

In spite of the fact they lived in a land that was large and rich, Americans, too, tasted the restrictions of the ration system. They obtained their tea and coffee, sugar and shoes, clothes and gasoline, and many other commodities only with their ration coupon. The money they possessed was no longer the most powerful medium of exchange, no longer stood alone as legal tender. Times without number, I watched men seek to bribe the butcher, or the grocer, or the service-station attendant to give them more than their share. If a rich man was honest, however, he received the same commodities of life as the poorest servant in his employ.

With the Japanese surrender on September 2, 1945, World War II came to a close. People turned their faces with hope toward the eastern sky, longing for the dawn of universal peace. They threw into the fire the ration coupon books that had bound them to limited provisions for so many years and heaved a sigh of relief. "Here's hoping," they said, "that we will never see this system again in our land."

With the dawn of 1973, rationing was once again in headlines all across America.

Fuel Shortage

On Friday morning, January 19, 1973, I was in Dallas, Texas. Picking up my copy of the Dallas *Morning News,* I read the bold headlines on the front page: FUEL SHORTAGE TURNING INTO CRISIS.

Later that day, the *Times-Herald* carried a similar headline: SHORTAGE OF HEATING OIL CAUSES NATIONAL CRISIS.

When in Charlotte, N.C. on May 10, 1973, I picked up the evening paper, The *Charlotte News,* and read the headline

9 FILLING STATIONS CLOSE,
GAS SHORTAGE LINK DENIED

Headlines of this nature were being seen more and more frequently in many areas of the nation.

In studying the various articles, I discovered that the announcement was received by many Americans with mingled consternation and confusion. One article read as follows:

> The national energy "crisis," here yesterday and gone tomorrow, seems almost elusive, and the experts disagree even on its existence. Now it seems the people directly affected by the current fuel shortages give different opinions, as two stories by Associated Press at left, and International Press at right, reflect. Is there an Energy Crisis? Facts are facts, but it depends on who you ask and when.

As I followed the reactions of our nation's leaders, I turned my eyes and interest again to the Dallas *Morning News,* January 16. The top half of 11-A was devoted to an article headlined, PRODUCERS ASK HIGHER GAS PRICES.

And on the bottom half of the same page, ran a second headline: KOSYGIN TOURS OIL GAS AREA IN USSR TO BOOST DEVELOPMENT PLANS.

The two stories on the same page did not come as a total surprise to some of us who had followed the developments of these events for several months. On November 12, 1972, I was in Eugene, Oregon. I picked up the daily paper, the *Register Guard,* and read an article reprinted from the Washington *Star,* which said,

> Washington *Star News* reports U.S. may buy as much as forty billion dollars' worth of natural gas from Russia during the next twenty-five years. U.S. companies

backed by federal financing would buy 36.5 trillion cubic feet of liquefied natural gas.

The head of one of the oil and gas producers' groups said Russian gas would cost six times more than the wholesale price of U.S. gas.

In response to that announcement in November, Tom Medders, Jr., head of the Independent Petroleum Association of America, said,

It is disturbing that our government is willing to encourage development of the Soviet Union's gas at such a cost when it is pursuing regulatory policies that are discouraging the needful capital expenditures to develop our own natural gas resources at home.

Serious-minded leaders, such as Senator Henry Jackson and Commerce Secretary Peter Peterson, and others, raised the question,

Would it not be unwise to make our nation dependent on an energy source that was held in the hands of a foreign nation?

In spite of the fact the alarms were being sounded, there was every indication that Americans would be subjected to gas rationing in the near future. Men as prominent as Mr. O'Leary, member of the Atomic Energy Commission, predicted rationing in the near future.

Russian Wheat

While America was discussing the purchasing of 36 trillion cubic feet of Russian gas, the Russians were occupied with the task of importing 20 million tons of wheat, which they had purchased from the United States, at a price of over $1 billion. Although the Russian press sought to keep this tremendous importation of wheat a secret from their own people, the free world was told it was because of a drought in the USSR.

Some indicated the drought in Russia was the worst in a hundred years, and affected 27.5 million acres of land.

Several years previously, I recalled reading an article by Sterling Slappey. His article carried the headline, SOVIET WHEAT PURCHASES LINKED TO ALCOHOL NEEDS.

Mr. Slappey quoted a report from the reputable German Institute of Industries. They declared the Soviets had greater need for wheat to distill into industrial alcohol than to turn into bread. They said that it took nine tons of wheat to make two tons of alcohol, which in turn would make one ton of synthetic rubber. They also declared the Russians needed 550,000 tons of industrial alcohol for the purposes mentioned. Some who read Slappey's article and his quotations from the Institute of German Industries, said,

> We do not mind as taxpayers subsidizing cheap wheat for Russian bread, but we would resent subsidizing the wheat purchase to the USSR if it were to be used for military production.

Was the fuel crisis in America genuine, or was it somehow linked to the possible purchase of Russian gas? If the suggested deal with Russia should develop as outlined, the 25-year contract for $40 billion worth of Russian gas would be the biggest transaction in the history of man.

Preparation for Shortage

Right or wrong, true or false, one thing seemed certain: the world was moving toward a ration system in the immediate future. Many people living only for the day awakened to the announced crisis with dismay. But others prepared for the future.

I remembered 1955 when I had returned to Europe from Africa. I paused to rest a few days in the little Swiss village of Beatenberg, nestled in the Alps, high above Thunersee. As I basked in the warm sunshine on the veranda of the Beau Regard Hotel, I was suddenly disturbed by a deep, rolling sound resembling thunder in the distance. My friend, Herr Bhent, owner of the hotel, surprised me with a strange explanation. The Swiss, he said, were storing wheat in preparation for the days of shortages that could be ahead.

I realized how typically Swiss this action was. By 1984, the world would have another billion mouths to feed, and what would that mean? It would require an *additional* 300 million tons of grain to feed another billion people. This would be more grain than was presently being grown by United States, Canada, and Western Europe combined.

In my youth, South America exported more grain than the United States and Canada. Now, because of her increased population, she was forced to import grain. China, too, had ordered 20 million bushels of wheat, and others were out shopping in the world markets.

The Black Horse

The prophet John described a dark hour coming on the earth when there would be shortage of food. In symbolical language, he likened this to a rider on a black horse, and wrote,

> And I beheld, and lo a black horse; and he that sat on him had a pair of balances in his hand. And I heard a voice . . . say, A measure of wheat for a penny . . . and see thou hurt not the oil.   (Rev. 6:5–6)

The Pale Horse

Following John's description of the black horse and famine, he described the rider on a pale horse:

And I looked, and behold a pale horse: and his
name that sat on him was Death.   (Rev. 6:8)

Often, after reading these words of John the Prophet, I
pondered the statements of some of our leading social
scientists and demographers. Dr. Paul Ehrlich, depart-
mental head of biological sciences at Stanford University,
had repeatedly addressed America on national television.
He spoke of the possibility of water being rationed in 1974.
He suggested that as many as 20 million may die of starvation in the next 12 months, and millions, if not billions,
perish with hunger in the near future.

Dr. Raymond Ewell served as vice-president of the
Research Department in the State University of New York.
He, also, portrayed a world where millions, if not billions,
would be starving to death within a very few years of time.

Danger of Famine – True or False?

While addressing the collective group of U.S. Army
chaplains in Europe on March 27, 1970, I alluded to the
remarks made by Dr. Ehrlich and Dr. Ewell. At the conclusion of my address, a veteran officer asked if I did not
think the comments concerning starvation were merely
propaganda. I asked the officer if he had ever been in Asia.
And he replied, no. "Then," I said, "sir, I am afraid you
have never seen poverty."

The chaplain had spent most of his years in America or
Western Europe. I reminded him that Western Europe
and Canada and America were in what we termed the food
belt of the world, which lies between latitudes 30 and 55.
Outside of the food belt, there are millions of acres of
steaming jungle, burning desert, and desolate mountain
waste. Some estimated that over 60% of the world's people
lived outside of the food belt.

Exploding Population

It was the poor nations of the world also that were facing the grim threat of a population explosion. This was a term seldom mentioned in my youth. Some felt the sudden emphasis on exploding population was propaganda produced by men in favor of a one-world government, in an effort to persuade that it was unite or perish. Those disturbed over exploding population painted a rather alarming picture, however:

A.D. 1 world population, ¼ billion
1850 world population, one billion
Today, 3.5 billion

The contrast between the past and present was impressive — 18 centuries for the world to grow from ¼ billion to one billion. Only 80 years required to add a second billion. Thirty years needed to add a third billion. A fourth billion would be added to world population in 14 years. That world population increase is 2% in one year does not sound disturbing. But to those who take time to ponder the true meaning, a world is seen with a population doubling every 35 years.

Demographers pointed out that the increase of population in the next 12 months would equal the combined populations of Canada, Australia, New Zealand, Switzerland, Israel, Denmark, Norway and Sweden.

I stared at the fire for a few minutes trying to comprehend what the future would hold if the increase in population should continue unabated. During the five hours I had been sitting by the fire, the world population had increased another 65,000. Doctor Harrison Brown of California declared if the population increase continued at its present rate, in seven centuries time there would literally not be standing room on the surface of the earth.

Naturally, the average American could not comprehend this. He lived in a land where there were fewer than a dozen people per square mile in some communities. He could not visualize the crowded congestion of Asia where some countries had an average of 700 people per square mile. Were the predictions overstated? Were they true or false?

I could not say for certain, but one thing I did know: I had walked the streets of Calcutta and of other cities of the East. I had seen the crowds of hungry people who had little or nothing of earthly goods and scarcely room to lay their head. Doctor Earl Butz, formerly of Purdue University, declared,

> I am convinced that most of the arable land of the world is now under cultivation. We have presently in our world about 3.3 billion acres suitable for food production. This represents about one acre per person at present, but in approximately three decades, the world population will double.

A Double Problem

Many naïve Americans, considering the population problem, say, "Technology will solve our crisis." But the more serious-minded point to the solemn facts that world food productivity is *declining,* not increasing. This, they declare, is the result of polluted air and water and impoverished soil.

When the ecologists met in Los Angeles, the *Los Angeles Herald Examiner* carried the headline, CAN HUMANITY SURVIVE FIVE YEARS?

It was most impressive to listen to the arguments of these scientific men. "Corn," they said, "does not grow in Iowa merely from what it draws from the soil or sod. It must receive its carbon from the carbon dioxide in the heavens above. To grow 100 bushels of corn, 20,000 pounds of carbon dioxide is required to provide the 5,500 pounds of carbon needed by the plants." I listened with interest to men discussing the delicate balance of the atmosphere which was: 78% nitrogen, 21% oxygen, with another dozen gases making up the 1% remaining. What happens, even in a land as big and free as America, when the people pour into the heavens annually:

> 100 million tons of carbon monoxide
> 32.2 million tons of sulfur oxide
> 32 million tons of hydrocarbon compounds
> 28.3 million tons of particulate matter
> 20.6 million tons of nitrogen oxide?

The result is death. I stood in the airport of Orlando, Florida, listening to a Floridian lamenting the loss of their pure air and pointing to the fact that the Spanish moss was already dying in the trees. I drove in the beautiful mountain range of Lake Arrowhead in California. The ranger pointed to the pine trees that were dying at the 5,000-foot level. The people of Denver, Colorado, feared they were losing their 400,000 elm trees, and in less than a decade, the people of Florida saw 15,000 palm trees die.

As I viewed the world picture and listened to the comments of the scientists, my thoughts turned again to the words of the prophet John. In Revelation 8:7, he spoke of a third part of the trees on earth dying:

The third part of trees was burnt up.

An astronaut predicted in 10 years' time the sun's rays would be diminished by 50% if man continued to pour into the heavens his ceaseless clouds of poison. But polluted air was not the only problem. Polluted water was equally alarming.

Water Pollution

Man poured into the oceans annually 7,422,000 tons of waste. This did not include the dredge spoils or the radioactive waste from plants along the shore. In a single year, America saw signs posted on 91 bathing beaches which read, "Unfit for Bathing" or "Closed Because of Pollution."

The problem was certainly not confined to America. It was worldwide. A traveler going abroad for the first time stared in wonder at warning signs placed in Hawaii, Samoa, Guam, Puerto Rico, and Europe; signs which read, "Polluted Water."

As I traveled over Europe, I was saddened to hear the beautiful Mediterranean referred to as "the sick sea" while up in the north of Europe, they spoke of the North Sea as the "Dying Sea."

Across the world, the sea life was sick and dying in many areas. Forty million dead fish were taken out of the Rhine River, poisoned with the 6,000 pollutants that were being poured into the waters of Europe's most picturesque and historical waterway. The *International Herald Tribune,* published in Europe, showed pictures of men in Amsterdam who had developed their photographs in the waters of the river. They declared there was enough acid in the water to develop film without adding any further chemicals. Similar pictures depicting like circumstances were published in faraway Japan. On the banks of Ascambia Bay in Florida, the big fishery was closed down. It was as dead as the sea life in the polluted waters. Men as prominent as Doctor Ripley predicted that the Pacific Ocean might be as devoid of life as Lake Erie in another two decades.

As I read these statistics, I turned again to the prophet John:

And the third part of the creatures which were in the sea, and had life, died.   (Rev. 8:9)

Fear of Pollution Drives Men to World Government

Not surprisingly, the leaders of the world viewed the conditions with concern. On December 3, 1968, leaders from Sweden introduced in the United Nations, Resolution 3298. They suggested pollution be solved through international agreement and cooperation. In 1970 the leaders of the world met in Strasbourg, France, to consider control of industry. In 1971, another meeting was conducted in Prague. On June 5, 1972, more than 1,200 delegates gathered in Stockholm, Sweden. They represented a hundred nations. They urged the government with global authority to police the nations of the world to save the planet from poison from pollution. Back in Washington, Richard Nixon declared in his address on the state of the union,

The threat to our environment demands action. It is literally now or never.

The Secretary-General of the United Nations was even more outspoken. In his address delivered in Texas he said,

We now face a worldwide crisis involving all living creatures.

Without doubt, the average man seemed to become more and more bewildered. When he turned his eyes to the heavens at noonday and saw nothing but the brown pall of ugly smog, he cried for laws that would clear the atmosphere and save him from the poison of pollution. The large oil refineries of America, failing to deliver the needed fuel and energy during the crisis weeks of 1973, declared one of the reasons for the shortage was the limitations imposed upon their production because of environmental control laws. Civic leaders accused the owners of the oil refineries of using the oil shortage as a deliberate influence to cause them to relax their environmental control. What could men do? Americans claimed they had lost $132 million in

their fruits and vegetable crops because of poisoned air.
Yet if they imposed laws strict enough to clear the atmosphere, then the economy was apparently endangered, and
the necessary production of oil and energy reached a crisis
point. The problem was not confined to the United States
alone. Countries as spacious as Canada were faced with
similar situations. In the city of Toronto, leaders forced 43
industries to close their operation for three days because
the pollution in Canadian skies had reached a crisis point.

Poison or Famine

Two ugly words had become part of modern man's
vocabulary, "poison" and "famine." Ugly as these words
appeared, I could not conceive an honest person pushing
them aside as mere propaganda of the one-world federalists.
Anyone discounting the dangers of pollution would indeed
have to close his eyes deliberately to the facts of the day. In
1941 there were 33 rivers in America which boasted of
salmon. Today there are six. Forest rangers told me of
lookout stations being simply abandoned, useless because
of the ugly pall of smog that hung so persistently over hills
and valleys.

An astronaut ventured to declare that already 50% of
the valuable rays of the sun were being denied to Mother
Earth by an ugly specter named pollution.

Could it be purely accidental that the prophet Amos long
ago wrote concerning this day and said,

I will darken the earth in the clear day.   (Amos 8:9)

Could it be mere chance that he added in the next breath,

I will send a famine in the land.   (Amos 8:11)

If the earth was being clouded with pollution, so were
the minds of men. As I pored over the comments made by

world-renowned scientists, their statements grew ever darker and more pessimistic. One wrote,

Mankind is racing toward extinction.

A group of British scientists published a so-called blueprint for survival. The central theme or thesis of their document read,

Growth in the world is self-defeating, and the planet cannot any longer sustain additional life. We are now moving toward social and biological collapse.

Certain people refuse to acknowledge such printed statements and brush them aside with disdain or deliberate disinterest. I could not. I was exposed too often to the confirmation of personal interviews and involvements with other men.

In Manchester, England, I spoke in the Free Trade Hall in the heart of the city. Not only were the hall's 2,500 seats filled, but another 1,200 persons gathered in the overflow Albert Hall across the street. I spoke on the words of the prophets and their description of our day, closing my address, as always, with the assurance that prophecy was not a doomsday message. It was a light in a dark place, promising a bright tomorrow and a permanent end to man's evils and woes.

On Sunday I said farewell to our Manchester audience, but remained in the city on Monday. That evening, one of Britain's best-known scientists, Dr. Robinson, spoke in the same hall. At the close of his address, his Manchester audience was left paralyzed with fear and deep despair. He offered them practically no hope for the future. On Tuesday morning, following his address, the *Manchester Guardian* carried the headline, DOCTOR ROBINSON, NEVER AGAIN VISIT MANCHESTER.

Dr. Robinson's words reminded me of those of Dr. René Dubos, Pulitzer Prize winner, retired microbiologist from Rockefeller University of New York, who said,

We used to speak of the atomic bomb as a threat. Now we might consider it as a relief.

Three ugly forces seemed to have suddenly arisen like giants on man's horizon: exploding population threatened famine, increased pollution threatened poison, atomic weapons threatened destruction. These three seemed to have joined in an unholy alliance to drive all of humanity into a one-world government. More and more men were turning in this direction as the only chance of survival. Even as the prophet had declared, men through fear would say "a federation, a federation."

The room in which I sat seemed to be aglow with the flames from the fireplace. The embers on the hearth that had warmed and cheered me now reminded me of the glow of atomic radiation.

10

The Earth Will Shake

ON AUGUST 6, 1945, the B-29 bomber known as the Enola Gay was flying in Japanese skies with the first atomic bomb to be dropped on mankind. Like most of the rest of the world, I was totally ignorant as to what was about to take place.

Early on that August morning, I had mounted a horse at Red Lodge, Montana, and had spent the day climbing Black Pyramid Mountain.

I had recently returned from visiting the disabled veterans who had come back from Okinawa and Iwo Jima. While the sound of the battle had died away in Europe, blood still flowed unceasingly in the Far Pacific regions. On the island of Iwo Jima, 4,590 American boys had died and 20,000 Japanese.

Saddened with the sorrows of war, I sought on this particular day to remove myself for a few hours from man's materialistic world and refresh my body and mind in God's great outdoors.

On top of Pyramid Mountain in the late August afternoon, I looked out across the valley with a sigh. How sad that men could not live in peace as the Creator intended them to live.

While I was standing alone in the silence of God's outdoor cathedral, the most fearful experience known to man was taking place in the Pacific.

A bomb a little larger than a football, weighing approximately 400 pounds, was dropped on the city of Hiroshima whose population was 343,969, and the whole world was shaken with the awful introduction of atomic destruction. Seven thousand acres of ground were scorched by the radiation of the blast. The Japanese newspaper, *Chugoku Shimbun,* estimated 280,000 Japanese were killed by the bomb, more than half the population of the city.

Late that evening when I drove into Billings, every channel of the news media was announcing the awful introduction to the atomic age.

Within three days, another atomic bomb was dropped — on the city of Nagasaki. Five days later Japan surrendered. War in the Pacific ended, but the mad arms race had only begun.

The atomic bomb was no accident that happened overnight. Over 40 years before the explosion in Japan, Einstein, a student in Switzerland, had told the scientific world that energy equaled MC^2. Most men chose to ignore his findings, and a few openly ridiculed his statement. How could one kilo of matter be equal to 25 billion kilowatt-hours of energy? But Einstein's theory was not a myth, and the fearful power of the universe had been discovered by man. Over $2 billion had been spent in research, developing a bomb capable of destroying man's world.

At my request, Colonel Garr went to Japan with his camera to document on film the destruction of Hiroshima. As he returned with the footage which we placed on the television stations of America, I was saddened at the sight of the destruction of life and property. Hiroshima had been scorched by the radiation of the blast. In the Peace Park at Hiroshima, the Japanese erected a memorial which read,

The mistake shall not be repeated.

The Atomic Bomb Race

The passing of time did little to substantiate the hopes of the Japanese.

September 23, 1949, Russia detonated an atomic bomb.

November 1, 1952, America exploded the first hydrogen bomb.

August 12, 1953, Russia released a hydrogen bomb.

May 15, 1957, Britain exploded an atom bomb.

February 13, 1960, France displayed her atomic power.

October 16, 1964, China joined the great powers possessing atom bombs.

The atomic scientists watched the buildup with dismay. In June, 1947, the *Bulletin of the Atomic Scientists* carried a picture on the cover with the clock of the world showing the hands reading eight minutes to midnight. In October, 1949, the same bulletin showed the same clock with the hands at four minutes to midnight. In March, 1950, the *Bulletin of the Atomic Scientists* magazine showed the clock with the hands at three minutes to midnight.

The Hydrogen Bomb

In San Diego, I talked with Captain Eddy. He had been with the expedition in the Marshall Islands on November 1, 1952, when America exploded her first hydrogen bomb. In a sober voice, Captain Eddy said, "No one could visualize the awfulness of that sight unless he were there in person." Two hundred miles above the Pacific, the mighty hydrogen bomb was detonated. The blast lighted up thousands of miles of Pacific sky. At Auckland, New Zealand, 3,800 miles away from the scene of the blast, New Zealanders said the ocean showed a reflection that was blood-red.

"The scientists present at the scene were dreadfully shaken," said Eddy. "They thought they had set the heavens aflame with a chain reaction of exploding atoms that would surely go around the world." On returning from his mission, Captain Eddy asked to be transferred to another department of service, and was given a position in the field of seismology, studying earthquakes back in the South Pacific.

Earthquakes and Atom Bombs

That there is a connection between atom bombs and earthquakes might sound humorous to some, but the facts allow little room for humor or ridicule.

On an island called Amchitka, southwest of Anchorage, Alaska, man sank a 53-inch shaft deep into the heart of the ground. On September 6, 1971, man created the largest man-made earthquake in history. The bomb he detonated in the island of Amchitka was 250 times more powerful than the one that had been dropped on Hiroshima. The explosion rocked not only the island of Amchitka; it caused the earth to tremor on the opposite side of the globe.

Professor Marcus Baath in Uppsala, Sweden, declared that the underground blast from Alaska caused his Richter scale to show a 7.4 earth tremor — *in Sweden.*

Increase of Earthquakes

Each year the United States government was spending $7.5 million on the study of earthquakes. The research revealed an amazing increase in earthquakes through the ages.

Fifteenth century — 150 recorded earthquakes
Sixteenth century — 153 recorded earthquakes
Seventeenth century — 378 recorded earthquakes
Eighteenth century — 640 recorded earthquakes
Nineteenth century — 2,119 recorded earthquakes

The twentieth century has broken all records of the past. In this century alone, more than a million people have died in earthquakes.

    Yugoslavia — 1,000 deaths
    Alaska — 114 deaths
    Chile — hundreds die
    Iran — 11,000 die
    Turkey — many killed by earthquakes
    Peru — 50,000 died in earthquakes

At Christmas of 1972, destruction and death was experienced in Managua, Nicaragua. One U.S. government report declared that by the year 2000, one out of four Americans will be living near an active earthquake fault.

The Great Earthquake of the Past

In past years, I have frequently paused to view the lava rock that covers much of western U.S.A. How could one explain the thousands of acres of lava rock in Eastern California, New Mexico, Arizona, Utah, Nevada, Wyoming, Nebraska, Eastern Washington, and Idaho? One day, surely, the face of Mother Earth must have broken and buckled in a thousand places while lava rock ran like rivers over much of the globe. The prophet Isaiah, in chapter 14, alludes to such an hour in the dim distant past when the earth trembled and became a desolate wilderness.

A Great Earthquake Still to Come

When describing the end of this age, Christ declared, "There shall be . . . earthquakes" (Matt. 24:7), earthquakes not comparable to anything of the past history, but a great earthquake even as described by John in his prophetic book of Revelation:

There was a great earthquake, such as was not since
men were upon the earth, so mighty an earthquake, and
so great . . . and the cities of the nations fell.
(Rev. 16:18–19)

John describes this earthquake in the same chapter in
which he discusses the battle of Armageddon and seemingly suggests when the heavens flame with atomic weaponry the earth will also reel and rock.

Scientists Warn of a Great Earthquake

With bated breath I reflected upon the statements of
certain scientific men suggesting that a salvo of bombs
exploded in the heavens above the surface of the earth
could well cause the entire globe to shake. True, they said,
the world weighs 6,600 billion times a billion tons. But it is
not dead weight. The earth that spins on its axis at 1,000
miles an hour also moves through space in its elliptical or-
bit around the sun at 67,000 miles an hour.

The great globe spinning on its axis in delicate balance
could be rocked and shaken by a fearful blast of atomic
weapons in the heavens, said the scientific group. This
seems to be exactly what the prophet Isaiah saw long ago
when he wrote,

The windows from on high are open, and the foundations of the earth do shake.   (Isa. 24:18)

And the writer of Hebrews adds,

Yet once more I shake not the earth only, but also
heaven.   (Heb. 12:26)

The Powers of the Heaven Shall Be Shaken

Apart from the war and danger of earthquakes, the atomic
bombs pose still another threat to man's survival on the
earth.

In May, 1966, I picked up a copy of *Science and Mechanics*, and read a feature article by A. I. Schutzer. It quoted men of scientific knowledge, such as Henry G. Houghton of M.I.T., who gave his report to the U.S. Senate. It also quoted Captain Howard T. Orville, former head of the President's advisory committee on weather control. In discussing radioactive fallout from atomic bombs, Captain Orville said, "The results could even be more disastrous than nuclear warfare."

Why would Captain Orville and Professor Henry Houghton, and men like Dr. Edward Teller express alarm over the weather patterns of the world being disrupted by man's detonating atomic bombs? The scientists pointed out that the earth's weather is manufactured in an envelope of atmosphere about eight miles high that encloses the world. The machine that makes the weather is the radiation that comes from the sun. Tamper with any one of the basic forces that mold our weather picture, said the scientists, and you change the weather somewhere in the world.

Why? First of all, because the amount of precipitation in the form of rain in any given area appears to be affected by the electrical balance between earth and air. The earth carries a negative charge. The air carries a positive charge. This is constantly being ionized by cosmic rays from the sun. Nature has set up an amazing system of re-balancing the positive-negative balance between earth and air. But, said the scientists, men seem to have upset this balance with the radioactive fallout.

As I moved across the world and kept interest in the changing weather patterns from nation to nation, the irregularities seemed endless. In 1965 for instance, for the first time to man's knowledge, four inches of snow fell in England in August. On the Tiber River in Rome, ice chunks were floating for the first time in over 500 years. While Russia was experiencing the worst drought in a century, torrential rains flooded eastern U.S.A. in 1972. Prior to 1945, the number of hurricanes and tornadoes in America averaged approximately 300 per year. Now, the number was almost double.

MANY NATIONS PLAGUED BY TOPSY-TURVY WINTER, read the headline in the January 6, 1973, edition of the *Los Angeles Times*. News media reported strange weather everywhere:

> Sweden warm, Israel cold, South Africa dry; flu-ridden Russia too balmy for crops. — "It was cold where it should have been warm, warm where it should have been cold, and dry where it should have been wet." — Europe is undergoing its most bizarre winter in recent times. — Drought-stricken South Africa has lost millions of dollars on crop loss. — Subtropical Israel lost $12 million in agriculture from unseasonable cold. — Crop losses in Rhodesia in the middle of the southern hemisphere summer have amounted to at least $30 million thus far. South African Agricultural Minister Hendrik Schoeman estimated crop losses at $318.5 million because of a three-month summer drought. — Norway, Sweden and Finland, normally blanketed by snow, all reported grass fires sparked New Year's Eve. Nils Tymark, Stockholm weather observer, said, "The situation is idiotic, I have never seen anything like it in all my life."

As I gathered data from the news media from the world relative to the disrupted weather patterns of the nations, and viewed them in the light of scientific statements made by men who felt it was brought about by the disruption of the balance in the atmosphere, I recalled the prophetic words of Christ:

> The powers of heaven shall be shaken.
>
> (Luke 21:26)

The most literal translation of this line from the original Greek reads,

The powers of the heaven shall be disrupted.

The Atomic Bomb — A Threefold Threat

When the first atomic bomb was dropped on August 6, 1945, man considered it only a weapon of war. Now men saw the atomic bomb threaten civilization in a threefold manner. There were indeed the dangers of destruction in war. To this had been added the scientific warnings that atomic explosions could disturb the balance of the globe and contribute to earthquakes, and thirdly, and not to be ignored, the disruption of the weather patterns of the world by pollution of radioactive fallout.

The Cry for World Government

Harold Urey said,

The only escape from total destruction of civilization will be a world government.

Robert J. Oppenheimer stated,

In the field of atomic energy, there must be set up a world power.

Arthur Compton added his word:

World government has become inevitable.

Dr. Ralph Barton Perry of Harvard said,

One-world government is in the making. Whether we like it or not, we are moving toward a one-world government.

Professor Hocking wrote,

Therefore the alternative is that we vest all political power in one agency and resign that power ourselves.

Today five nations alone have amassed over fifty thousand atomic weapons. When President Nixon was asked by a news writer about his attitude toward Russia's superiority in the heavy missile race, he replied,

Gentlemen, we have enough weapons already stockpiled to destroy several civilizations such as this.

And before him, President Johnson had said,

In the event of a nuclear war between Russia and America, 100 million Americans and 100 million Russians would be dead in the first nuclear exchange. The great cities would be in ashes, and the fields would be barren. The industrial world would be destroyed, and man's dreams vanished.

One-Man Government?

I sat in Brussels in March, 1972, with my friend, Dave Oliver, who had devoted 28 years of his life to tirelessly working with the Atomic Energy Commission. In recalling the first atomic bomb dropped on Hiroshima on August 6, 1945, we were impressed that it was the voice signal of the U.S. President, Harry Truman, that released that bomb from the B-29 that flew over Hiroshima on that memorable day. With knowledge of that amazing incident, we turned in the prophetic Scriptures to the prophecies of John in the book of Revelation. Here the prophet not only spoke of a one-world government, canceling the old monetary currencies of the past and establishing a new number system, the prophet also spoke of a world leader, having authority over the military power of the world, and declared,

Power was given him over all kindreds, and tongues, and nations [and he adds], He maketh fire come down from heaven on the earth in the sight of men.

(Rev. 13:7, 13)

If a man became head of a world government and possessed such power, surely it would be greater than what any man in history had ever possessed before him.

What would happen if such power was invested in a man who should turn into a maniac like Adolph Hitler? Was there such a danger? Of course there was, and most sober-minded leaders of government realized it. But man seemed to be caught between two undesirable alternatives. The old paths behind him pointed back to Hiroshima, Nagasaki, and 50 million dead from World War II. The other path offered the forfeiture of rights by individuals and nations being pushed daily nearer to a form of world government.

Grenville Clark said,

Perhaps it may take a few nuclear bombs and several million deaths.

And Joseph Clark added,

The people will follow when the leaders tell them there is no alternative.

11

Two Man-Made Solutions: Communism and the UN

TIME and again, man had sought to establish his temple of peace. There was the Tribunal Palace in the Hague. For weeks, we had lived on Scheveningsweg in the shadow of the Peace Palace. To walk in its echoing corridors was to be impressed that it resembled a mausoleum more than a monument.

Then there was the League of Nations established in Geneva at the close of World War I. Forty-six nations participated there at the cost of $190 million before its final demise in 1946. From the ashes of destruction and the blood of the beachheads, man turned his face to San Francisco's Golden Gate, hoping to build on American shores an organization that would guarantee peace to the world.

The Birth of the UN

It was a beautiful June day in San Francisco in 1945. The flags were flying and a stiff breeze was blowing in from the Pacific. I watched the delegates from 50 nations gather in the world's most important meeting. Over 50 million had been left dead on the battlefields of the world. With smoke still rising from the ruined cities of Europe and Asia, and tears still wet on the cheeks of widows and orphans, the delegates of the world sat around the peace tables to discuss one more attempt at universal peace.

One American delegate asked if it would be in order to suggest prayer, asking God's guidance on the opening with an invocation. His suggestion was immediately brushed aside by those who stated it would be offensive to the atheistic delegates who had congregated for the meeting.

When Woodrow Wilson, supported by many young intellectuals of America, had sought to influence the U.S. government in 1920 to support the League of Nations, he failed. Why, then, 26 years later, were American people ready to join the United Nations, which, in a sense, was the tree that grew from the roots of the League of Nations?

Men pointed out that the two obstacles which prevented America from joining the League of Nations were old-fashioned ideas pertaining to patriotism and religion. In the book entitled *Great Ideas Today: 1971,* published by the *Encyclopaedia Britannica,* Joseph Clark says,

> Old fashioned patriotism is surely an obstacle to world government.

But the so-called old-fashioned ideas of patriotism and religion seemed to be waning in America. By a vote of eight to one, the Supreme Court expressed their disfavor toward compulsory prayer in the public schools, and with a vote of six to one denied students public Bible reading in the classroom.

When a survey was made of 1,150 high school students, only one in 39 could name three books written by Saint Paul. Only one student in 38 could name three Old Testament prophets. Only one in 8 could name three of the Ten

Commandments. A survey made in the colleges showed 60% could not name one parable that was delivered by Jesus, and 53% of Americans were unable to name even one of the Four Gospels.

Russia was spending more than a billion dollars on literature and propaganda outside of the USSR each year. The doctrines of socialism were not only being taught in the classrooms of the colleges, but were also being heard from the pulpits of many churches, and from the pens of religious leaders.

I wonder, I said to myself, how many Americans have studied the charter of the UN sufficiently to realize that it commits each member nation to a program of total socialism for itself and for all other nations. Alger Hiss was a major architect of the UN charter and served as the secretary general of the San Francisco conference for the organization of the United Nations. Twenty-five years later, U Thant was quoted praising Lenin as a political leader whose ideals were reflected in the United Nations' charter.

Wealth and Poverty

Why, I asked myself repeatedly, did so many American leaders, both in church and in the classroom of the college, speak strongly in favor of world socialism? E. Stanley Jones, in his *The Choice Before Us,* declared,

> God reached out and put his hand on the Russian Communist. Communism is the only political position that really holds the Christian position.

In one sense, I found it very difficult to comprehend a man like E. Stanley Jones writing lines that seemed to endorse Communism.

On the other hand, I reminded myself of the years that he had spent in India. In 1953, speaking for many days on the club grounds of Lucknow, I saw the results of this man's work in that city of north central India. Undoubtedly Jones was moved by the scenes of squalor and poverty that plagued the masses of that great nation. He must have contrasted the poor and the hungry with the abnormal wealth of such men as the Nizam of Hyderabad, a descendant of the Mogul emperors, who ruled over 15 million poverty-stricken subjects for decades. Reputedly, he had more wealth than any other man in the world, with a net income of $15 million annually. Much of his wealth came from the fabulous valley of Golconda, one of the world's richest diamond mines.

The Nizam had 500 wives, and he gave his favorite one a gold Rolls Royce. He ate all of his meals off golden plates, and boasted that the English displayed 24 golden plates in London, while he had golden place settings for 150 guests. One of his favorite diamonds was the 182½-carat diamond that he used for a paperweight. He sat in chairs and relaxed on couches of solid gold, and had a carriage of gold built that was not usable because of its weight.

If Stanley Jones endorsed socialism, it was perhaps because he had stood among the beggars and hungry children in the shadow of the Taj Mahal. It was without doubt the most beautiful tomb in the world. It was built by the Indian ruler, Shah Jahan, as a memorial to his favorite wife, Muntaz-i-Mahal, which means "Bride of the Palace." It took 20,000 workmen 21 years to erect the Taj, and when the workmen finished the delicate tasks of carving their marble and alabaster into 70-foot domes rising 150 feet high, they undoubtedly gazed at the slender minarets, supposedly built as towers for prayer, mirrored in the reflecting pools beside the tomb, and then turned to Shah Jahan for their reward. Did he give them a smile of appreciation or a hand of gratitude? No, the payment they received for creating one of the beauties of the world was the ugly point of the soldier's knife that pierced their eyes. Shah Jahan wanted to make sure no other monarch would ever again have a Taj as beautiful as his.

Communism in Egypt

If there were Communists in Egypt, it, too, might be understandable. The Great Pyramid of Gizeh served as a perpetual reminder of the days when masters with a stroke of the whip compelled men to serve them as slaves. As I climbed the Great Pyramid, and walked around its perimeter, my mind seethed with a thousand questions. How could this monument be built on desert sand, towering 484 feet high, with a base that measured 761 feet? Where could they have quarried the granite which they had piled in 201 concourses, some blocks of granite weighing as much as twenty tons?

Some felt the immense blocks of granite were brought from Syene, a distance of 500 miles. The total weight of the pyramid was estimated to be 6 million tons. A mathematician calculated that the volume of the pyramid was 85 million cubic feet. Should a monument as large as the pyramid be converted into a wall four feet high and one foot thick, it would extend from New York City to San Francisco.

The ancient record tells us that 100,000 men, laboring in relays of three months, worked 30 years to complete the Great Pyramid. Were modern engineers to build such a monument today, the contract price would be over $5 billion.

Men might be able to compute the weight and the measurements of the Pyramid, but they would never be able to measure the cries and the tears of the laborers who bore the heavy burdens and built the monument on the desert sand, only to pass and be forgotten by everyone but God.

Communism in Germany

While in the Alps of Southern Germany, I visited the beautiful palace built by Ludwig of Bavaria. "He was a genius," said our guide, with a touch of German pride. "The fountain that erupts in the reflecting pool in front of the palace is the product of Ludwig's ingenuity. He captured the mountain stream far back in the hills and brought it down to the reflecting pool to erupt in regular intervals like a giant geyser." The genius of Ludwig was equally displayed inside the palace. The dining-room table was prepared for his own self-indulgence. He preferred to eat in total solitude. A touch of a button lowered the table to a room below where the waiters and chefs loaded it with the various dainties of the land. Another touch of the button brought the table back up to the king, who preferred to live in a fantasy world.

"He was a dreamer," said our guide. "He seemed detached from the people of his land." I walked through another castle built by Ludwig. It was called the Neuschwanstein. From room to room I wandered, beholding the beauty, and contemplating the genius of this man who built this castle with the symbol of the swan, which had been the theme of Wagner's composition. In one room was Wagner's personal piano, a gift to the king, who had been an admirer of the great composer. And what happiness did Ludwig derive from all of this? Enough to cause him to take his own life in a lonely mountain lake. In order to build his dream castles, he had taxed the Bavarians so unmercifully that they scarcely had money for food.

In the bright Bavarian sunlight, I could see the Neuschwanstein shining majestically in the green forest and outlined against the sky. And yonder in the distance, I could see a tiny lake, the last resting-place of a leader who dedicated his life to serving himself, rather than his people.

The Story of the Ages

The story of the ages changes little. With monotonous repetition it reveals the struggles between the poorest of the poor, and the richest of the rich. When Attila of the Huns was buried in Hungary, he had his body encased in a coffin of gold, a second coffin of silver, and a third coffin of iron. In the midst of a vast plain, a host of prisoners dug a huge grave and buried him in the night. His coffin was covered with spoils and the riches from many nations, and when all was finally and carefully hidden underground, the workmen were murdered so that the resting place of the king might never be known.

The same procedure was basically followed at the death of Alaric, the all-conquering Goth, who conquered Rome. At his death, multitudes of captives were set to work to turn the mighty river out of its course. When this was done, they laid the tyrant in a huge sepulcher adorned with the spoils and trophies of vanquished armies. They buried him in the river bed, and then turned the waters again in their natural course, so that all might be hidden from view. These workmen, too, were put to death, so that the location of the grave of the tyrant would be kept a secret.

On the banks of the Thames, I visited the Tower of London. It was begun in the year 1000, and the British had filled it with valuable things belonging to every age. The Tower of London had beheld some of the bitterest tragedies in history. In the Tower, kings and princes, queens and princesses had been murdered. Great and good men were imprisoned, tortured, and killed. Had Gundulf the Weeper known what a place of agony he was creating, when he built the Tower, he would have wept still more and with far better reason.

I stood with an endless line of tourists watching men and women with eager faces gaze with excitement on the gold and jewels that had been gathered for the Empire. My mind went back through history, recalling vividly some of the events of the past and the names of the famous men that had come down as immortal from Britain's golden age. There was Francis Drake, who, to the British of his day, was the greatest hero of all.

On the high seas, Drake, time and again, challenged the mighty ships of Spain. Time after time, he set their towering ships aflame. In his own ship, the *Golden Hind,* he brought back to England $200 thousand worth of gold.

From years of traveling abroad, I turned my thoughts again to my homeland where so many were preaching the doctrine of socialism. The American public, according to H. R. Gross, was in debt to the tune of $1.7 trillion, which means that every child born a U.S. citizen inherits the equivalent of a personal debt of $8,500.

Some pointed to the weaknesses of Capitalism and declared that Communism was preferable. Some uninformed speakers and writers suggested that the leaders and founders of Communism had a love for the laborer and were seeking to build a wonderful world of brotherly love. Was this true? There was only one way to find out: examine the records.

Marx

Because Karl Marx is considered to be one of the early fathers of Communism, I became interested in learning what I could about his own early life. Carl Schurz, a political leader of the nineteenth century, wrote concerning Marx,

I have never seen a man whose bearing was so provoking and intolerable. . . . Everyone who contradicted him, he treated with abject contempt. It is said of those who knew Marx that he hated people as individuals.

Stalin

Svetlana Alliluyeva, the daughter of Joseph Stalin, writes on pages 140–42 of her book *Only One Year,**

Twenty-seven of those years I lived under a heavy weight . . . a time of singlehanded despotism, bloody terror, economic hardships, the cruelest of wars, and ideological reaction. . . . I lived at the very top of the pyramid, where truth hardly reached one at all. . . . In the family in which I was born and bred nothing was normal, everything was oppressive, my mother's suicide was most eloquent testimony to the hopelessness of the situation. Kremlin walls all around me, secret police in the house, in the kitchen, at school. And over it all a wasted, obdurate man, fenced in from his former colleagues, his old friends, from all those who had been close to him, in fact from the entire world, who with his accomplices had turned the country into a prison, in which everyone with a breath of spirit and mind was being extinguished; a man who aroused fear and hatred in millions of men—this was my father.

The leaders of Communism make no effort to conceal their attitude toward truth. Lenin said,

Promises are piecrusts, made to be broken,

and

The best revolutionary is a youth without morals.

Joseph Stalin said,

Honest diplomacy is as impossible as iron wood or dry water.

When Dwight D. Eisenhower was in office as President, he declared in a State of the Union message,

---

* Harper & Row, 1969.

We have learned the bitter lesson that international agreements, historically considered by us as sacred, are regarded in Communist doctrine and practice to be mere scraps of paper.

Communism and God

The attitude of Marx and Lenin toward God was clearly expressed in the language,

I hate all gods.

Karl Marx declared,

The idea of God is the keystone of a perverted civilization. It must be destroyed.

This attitude seemed to permeate all who embraced the doctrines of Communism. Khrushchev's son-in-law, Alexei Adzhubei, said,

Every flirtation with God is an unutterable abomination.

All who read the words of Lenin were indeed aware of his hatred of God and religion. He wrote,

Religion is the opium of the people. Religion is a kind of spiritual gin, in which the slaves of capitalism drown their human shape and their claim to any decent human life.

Communism and the Home

Long ago God gave to Moses the Ten Commandments. These became the foundation stones of all advanced civilization of the western world. One of those commandments read,

Honour thy father and thy mother: that thy days may be long upon the land which the Lord thy God giveth thee.   (Exod. 20:12)

Repeatedly, Moses reminded the people of this solemn command from the Almighty (e.g., Deut. 5:16). Christ, too, repeatedly referred to this commandment, and Paul, in writing to the Ephesian church, said,

Children, obey your parents in the Lord: for this is right. Honour thy father and mother; which is the first commandment with promise; That it may be well with thee, and thou mayest live long on the earth.

(Eph. 6:1–3)

The words of Moses, Jesus, and Paul were in direct contrast to those of the *Communist Manifesto:*

The bourgeois clap-trap about the family and education, about the hallowed co-relation of parent and child becomes all the more disgusting.

Paul in writing to Titus concerning motherhood said,

Teach the young women . . . to love their husbands, to love their children, to be . . . keepers of the home.

(Titus 2:4–5)

Communism and Their Enemies

Jesus said,

I say unto you which hear, Love your enemies, do good to them which hate you, Bless them that curse you, and pray for them which despitefully use you. And unto him that smiteth thee on the one cheek offer also the other.   (Luke 6:27–29)

Marx and Engels stated in the *Communist Manifesto,*

Their ends can be attained only by the forceable overthrow of *all* existing social conditions.

During the Stalin purges, it is estimated that 374 generals and 30,000 line officers were put to death.

Dr. Nicholas Zermov, professor at the University of Moscow, declared,

Four or five million Christians perished since the Revolution (not including those put to death for political reasons).

Zermov also said that in 1935 the government closed 14,000 churches and convicted 3,687 clergymen in criminal courts. Some of these were executed by firing squads.

China's record was no better. On October 1, 1949, Mao, in order to crush resistance on the home front, ordered what he called Mass Shock, in which 12 million were wiped out. (Western statistics put the number at 20 million.)

In February, 1950, Mao called all identified with the previous national government to register. They were promised forgiveness. Three months later they were the victims of a mass purge.

Communism and the Weak

In writing to the Romans, the apostle Paul said,

We then that are strong ought to bear the infirmities of the weak, and not to please ourselves.   (Rom. 15:1)

In contrast, Joseph Stalin said,

In our time it is not our custom to give any consideration to the weak.

On March 26, 1959, Peter Chu Pong, former Minister of Nanking, China, appeared before the House Committee on Un-American Activities, and testified:

We were placed in classes for brainwashing. From morning till night, they taught Communism. They wanted me to reject Christ and give up the church and admit that the only God was Mao-Tse-tung, head of the Communistic Government.

A former Communist said,

They asked me to forget Katyn Forest. Forget the slave labor camps, forget the genocide of the captive nations, forget the butchery of Budapest, forget the annihilation of 30 million people, forget their anti-God, anti-Christ, anti-church, and anti-home doctrines, and to forget all that is dear and place our faith in them.

With amazing courage some of Russia's finest writers have dared to express the true feelings of their hearts.

Alex Solzhenitsyn, considered by many to be Russia's greatest author writes,

The USSR is guilty of committing *spiritual murder,* a variant of the gas chamber but more cruel.

In an edition of the Los Angeles *Times* in April, 1973, Murray Seeger tells how the government leaders in Russia seek to control men's minds and spirits. He describes the heavy volume of anti-religious action and propaganda which have been continued in all parts of Russia against many different faiths ever since the Bolshevik Revolution took place 55 years ago.

In light of the Communist attitude toward Christians and Jews, are men not justified in asking why this government should receive favored treatment?

Why should American taxpayers pay $300 million in taxes to subsidize cheap wheat for the USSR? Or why should Russia get 200,000 tons of butter from The European Common Market for 20 cents per pound, when the British pay 60 cents for the same butter?

Perhaps some of the international bankers might shed some light on this. They might tell us how the Communist banks were able to borrow 40 billion Eurodollars six months before the dollar was devalued 10% on February 6th of 1973, and comment on the extraordinary good fortune of their timing. For when this debt is repaid, it will be repaid with dollars valued at 90 cents, which means a net profit of $4 billion for the borrowers.

"Only one thing is clear," wrote one economist from Europe, "and that is the mystery that surrounds these strange actions."

That Russia was receiving favored treatment was beyond any question. It had been, ever since the birth of the United Nations. When it was organized in 1945, there were only 50 nations of the world represented in the UN. In the 10 years following its birth, however, Communism had spread across the world at the rate of 44 square miles per hour.

As new nations were being born and being admitted to the UN, the roster clearly revealed the young and struggling nations being admitted were often those who had accepted the doctrines and principles of Communism. This doctrine thrived especially in undeveloped areas, estimated to be at least 72% of the whole.

With the apparent domination of Communistic personalities in control of UNESCO and the International Police Force, reflected in the UN charter, it was difficult to understand how the United States could be removed much further from the position of leadership.

In the 21 years following the establishment of the UN there were 22 presidents of UN General Assembly. Not one was an American. The same could be said about the highest office, that of Secretary-General.

Representation in the UN

As I sat by the fire on this particular evening, allowing memory to take me back through the milestones that man had passed in his momentum toward a one-world government, I pondered the possibilities of the United Nations holding supreme control of the entire world. If 95% of the world's population was already in the UN and other nations such as East and West Germany were to be admitted, it had already reached the place of world representation. But was it capable of bringing man what man most desired, world peace and order?

I stood once in the general assembly hall in the UN and counted the number of seats being filled with the respective nations of the world, trying to estimate the population of the various countries. There was Iceland and Barbados whose population was smaller than that of Albuquerque, New Mexico.

There was Luxembourg and Swaziland, Fiji and Gabon, whose populations were less than that of Columbus, Ohio.

Cyprus and Kuwait had populations smaller than Louisville, Kentucky.

Mauritania, Jamaica, and Mongolia had fewer people than Houston, Texas.

Costa Rica and Nicaragua, Albania, Sierra Leone, Somalia, Dahomey, Honduras, had populations only half of that of Philadelphia, Pennsylvania.

No one in honesty or kindness would want to exclude or deny a small nation its rightful place. But serious-minded people are prone to ask whether it is fair for nations as small as these to have a vote in the General Assembly of the UN which would equal the vote of the United States with over 200 million people. Did the vote in the General Assembly of the UN really represent the people of the world with equity?

The Financial Record of the UN

When the United Nations chose to place its headquarters on the banks of the Hudson River in New York, the American government loaned $65 million tax-free toward the center. John D. Rockefeller, Jr., gave $8 million toward the land. The City of New York gave $26.5 million to prepare the site. The Ford Foundation gave over $6 million toward a library to contain 400,000 books. Within a quarter of a century, the expenditures of the United Nations reached $9.2 billion. Of this amount, the United States has provided 41%. The financial records in a single year revealed Americans paid 31.8% of the annual UN budget.

The picture grew more discouraging when one gazed at the financial records of a single year and saw that Russia was $66.9 million in the red. Apparently not content to have the United States carry the heavy financial burden of the United Nations, the Russians wanted her to do even more. On Friday, November 17, 1972, the *Los Angeles Times* carried an article which read,

> Russia urges U.S. to increase UN aid. The normally humdrum budgetary committee broke into oratorical fireworks. . . . V. S. Safronchuk speaking to the General Assembly said, "The U.S. should be assessed 38.4% instead of its present 31.52%." This brought U.S. Ambassador George Bush to his feet; pointing to Safronchuk, Bush asserted that his government pays 40% of the overall costs, those outside as well as inside the regular budget, compared with the Soviet's contribution of 7%.

A look at the program within the UN that was supposed to be carried on as a humanitarian effort for the needy of the world—UNICEF (United Nations International Children's Emergency Fund)—revealed in 1970 that Russia gave $5.2 million compared to America's $159 million. This meant that Russia gave 1.47% compared to America's 45%.

Where, I asked myself, were the men who said the doctrines of Communism were closest to those of the early church Christians? If the early church shared things in common, it was with the spirit of love which said, What I have is yours. But the doctrine of Marx and Lenin was as different from Christianity as darkness is from light. Their spirit of greed and selfishness declared, What you have is mine, and if you do not give it freely, we will take it from you by force.

The Justice of the United Nations

Foundations of the United Nations were laid by the United States, the United Kingdom, and the Soviet Union, from August 21 to September 28, 1944, in the Dumbarton Oaks Conference in Washington. Immediately afterward, the Republic of China became one of the five founding nations, and was given lifetime membership in the Security Council. Her population was larger than ¾ of the nations who held membership in the UN. Even in Taiwan, she maintained diplomatic relationship with 60 countries of the world. In the field of commerce, she exported over a billion dollars' worth of merchandise annually, and yet when Albania, with a population half the size of Philadelphia, made a motion that the Republic of China be expelled, the smaller nations rallied to the suggestion in a demonstration of emotionalism and bias that left a permanent blemish on the record of the UN. Ambassador Bush said on October 25, 1971, "Never have I seen such hate."

The late David Lawrence, respected news journalist and editor of the *U.S. News & World Report,* said, "Can any nation be safe in an atmosphere of such irresponsible and emotional action?"

The Chinese leaders returned to Taiwan in tears. They carried with them a record free from blot or blemish. Their dues had been paid. Their position had been held with honor. But without a single grievance against them, they were expelled and not even granted the courtesy of being permitted to speak for themselves. Someone dared to sug-

gest before their departure that perhaps Communist China
and Nationalist China could each have a seat. The pro-
Communist block pounded their desks and shouted down
the proposal. A few days later, they were willing to talk
about two seats being given to both West Germany and
Communist East Germany, to sit side by side.

The UN and Peace

When asked if the UN hoped to end all wars, international lawyer Ambassador J. Reuben Clark, Jr., said,

> There seems no reason to doubt that such real ap-
> proval as the Charter has among the people is based
> upon the belief that if the Charter is put into effect,
> wars will end. . . . The Charter will not certainly end
> war. The Charter provides for force to bring peace,
> but such use of force is itself war. . . . The Charter
> does take from us the power to declare war and to
> choose the side on which one must fight.

If men hoped the United Nations would bring peace to
the world, their hopes proved groundless. The list of wars
fought since 1945 seemed almost endless:

Indonesia, 1945–1947
China, 1945–1949
Kashmir, 1947–1949
Greece, 1946–1949
Israel, 1948–1949
Philippines, 1948–1952
Indo-China, 1945–1954
Malaya, 1945–1954
Korea, 1950–1953
Formosa, 1950
Kenya, 1952–1953
Sinai, 1956

Suez, 1956
Hungary, 1956
Quemoi-Matsu, 1954–1958
Lebanon, 1958
Tibet, 1950–1959
Cyprus, 1955–1959
Algeria, 1956–1962
Cuba, 1958–1959
Laos, 1959
Kuwait, 1961
Goa, 1961
Yemen, 1962
Congo, 1960–1962
Cuba, 1961
South Vietnam, 1959–1973
Himalayas, 1959–1962
Angola, 1960
West Guinea, 1962
Colombia, 1960
Cuba, 1962
Algeria-Morocco, 1963
Venezuela, 1963
Malaysia, 1963
Congo, 1964
Thailand, 1964
Dominican Republic, 1965
Peru, 1965
Pakistan, India, 1965–1972

On August 10, 1962, Herbert Hoover said,

I urged the ratification of the United Nations by the
Senate, but now we must realize the United Nations
has failed to give us even a remote hope of lasting

peace. Instead it adds to the dangers of wars, which now surround us.

The United Nations and God

What has been the attitude of the United Nations toward God? Dr. Julian Huxley, who had served as Director of UNESCO, said,

While a faint trace of God still broods over the world like the smile of a cosmic Cheshire cat, science and knowledge will soon rub that trace away.

UN Leaders Ask for More Power

On August 23, 1970, U Thant addressed the Fourteenth World Congress of World Association of World Federalists in Ottawa, Canada, and said,

A world under law is realistic and obtainable. The ultimate crisis before the UN is the crisis of authority.

The convention conducted by the lawyers and judges of the world in the interest of world law was a solemn sight indeed. There were 263 judges from every continent, Africans in red robes, sitting by Indians and Pakistanis, and Israelis, and 5 justices from the U.S. Supreme Court. Even a copy of the Magna Carta was on hand. And banners across the platform read "Pax Orbis ex Jure," meaning "World Peace by World Law."

There were 119 countries represented. The main decision was to recommend that the UN Charter be amended to provide compulsory jurisdiction for individuals, as well as nations. Joseph Clark called for,

an executive with substantially greater powers than those now exercised by the Secretary-General of the UN. A judiciary system modeled after the world court. Decisions enforced by a world police force, under the command of a world executive.

Would man be willing to resign such power to the United Nations, knowing it was under Communistic domination? For many the answer was *yes*. One person said,

> If the price of avoiding all-out thermal nuclear wars should prove to be acquiescence in the Communistic domination of the world, it seems probable that such a price would be paid.

And if the question was asked, "Why?" perhaps the answer would best be expressed by Adlai Stevenson, who in a speech to the United Nations Correspondents' Association said,

> Interpret us . . . as puzzled, yet aspiring men, struggling on the possible brink of Armageddon.

Why would men who are members of a strong and a free democracy vote in favor of a world organization which would include the explosive characteristics of South America, the turbulence of the Middle East, the tyranny of Russia, and the violence of Asia? One speaker answered the question by saying sadly,

> No, it is not desirable; but we have no alternative. There is no other way out.

12

The March Toward Armageddon

TIME and again America sought to reduce her military strength and atomic weaponry. But they found that the formula did not work. It was impossible to disarm for peace.

On the evening of Tuesday, May 27, 1969, I went to the postbox in front of our Washington home, and picked up the newspaper, *The Evening Star*. The entire back page was devoted to an article by Secretary of Defense Melvin Laird and others, entitled, THE REAL TRUTH ABOUT HOW MANY U.S. SENATORS ARE BEING TRICKED BY RUSSIA.

The subtitles were equally startling:

Russia is racing to a five-to-one first-strike nuclear superiority over America. Here is how they tricked America into letting it happen . . . and how they are now tricking many U.S. Senators into leaving us defenseless.

In 1958, the United States had a five to one nuclear superiority over Russia. To keep its lead, the U.S. was testing bigger and bigger nuclear bombs, and so was Russia. Suddenly Russia announced she would like a moratorium on these tests. Radiation fallout was alarming the world, so the U.S. and Russia agreed to explode no more test bombs in the air. In the spirit of that moratorium, the U.S. began dismantling its testing installations, and stopped developing bigger bombs.

Russia did just the opposite. It secretly raced ahead. Suddenly, in September, 1961, Russia violated the moratorium with a series of tests in which it exploded the world's biggest hydrogen bomb, an incredible hundred-megaton monster vastly more powerful than anything the U.S. had. Overnight, Russia went years ahead of the U.S. in vital knowledge.

Tricked and dismayed, the U.S. then negotiated the famous test-ban treaty. It was approved by the U.S. Senate. President Kennedy acclaimed a new era of successful cooperation between the two countries. In that spirit, the U.S. started cutting back on our missiles, taking the largest ones out of our stockpiles.

Russia again did just the opposite. It raced ahead. Suddenly, in June, 1967, a special study ordered by the Congress showed that while the U.S. had gone backward, the Soviets had forged ahead in total megatonnage.

By April of 1973, *U.S. News & World Report* showed Russian supremacy in many areas of the arms race:

Intercontinental Ballistic Missiles

USSR	USA
1,590	1,054

Surface-to-Air Missiles

USSR	USA
10,000	500

Nuclear Missile Submarines

USSR	USA
48	41

Interceptor Aircraft

USSR	USA
3,000	600

Anti-Ballistic Missile Systems

USSR	USA
64	0

So forboding was the prospect of atomic annihilation that many people sought to build around the sensitivities of their inner soul an insulation of indifference. But they could not shut entirely from their minds the sobering truths of their day. Dope addiction became rampant across the nation. The younger generation, seemingly in hopeless despair, sought to drown their normal sensitivities in a sea of hallucinogens. Yes, the arms race would continue unabated.

For years I had followed with interest efforts made by leaders of Russia and America in the SALT Talks. After endless months and thousands of dollars had been spent in these discussions, suddenly the Strategic Arms Limitations Talks became virtually meaningless, because China had reached the place where she too had become a major atomic power threat.

Senator Stuart Symington, addressing the Senate Armed Services Committee on January 9, 1973, said,

China is expected in 1975 to have an operational intercontinental ballistic missile which could be capable of striking the U.S. . . . I was shocked to find out how close another power is to becoming a super-power in missiles. This to me reduces the practical effect of the Strategic Arms Limitations Talks with the Soviet Union.

It seemed that the entire world was on the march toward Armageddon and knew it. I picked up a copy of the

Reader's Digest and read thirteen references to the battle of Armageddon. On the cover of the *Post,* one word was splashed across the front of the bright red cover: ARMA-GEDDON. At a newsstand on the streets of Barcelona, Spain, I picked up a newspaper with the bold headline discussing Armageddon. In his dying hours, Douglas MacArthur said,

We are now entering Armageddon.

Vietnam

Weary of war and fearing for his future, man was willing to cling to any thin thread of hope. Willing, indeed, he was to sit in the tension-filled halls of the UN and indulge in the divisive arguments which continued endlessly between the opposing blocks of power. For 10 years, the nations had discussed the war in Vietnam with bitter accusations, while presidential envoy Henry Kissinger traversed a well-beaten path between Peking, Moscow, Washington, and Paris to obtain an uneasy peace.

The years had taken a tremendous toll of American life and property. Reportedly, 304,000 American boys had been wounded, and 56,000 had been killed. Since 1966, America had dropped 7.1 million tons of bombs on Vietnam. She had lost 1,647 planes and 2,281 helicopters. The war had cost as much as $70 million per day to wage. Arthur Burns, referred to as the boss of the Federal Reserve, estimated the tangential price.

World War I

I was too young to remember another peace, earlier in the century, the end of "the war that was to end all wars." The armistice was signed on the eleventh hour of the eleventh day of the eleventh month in the year, bringing to a close the fearful struggle of World War I.

I was two years old on that fateful day in 1918. Spending the first 12 years of my life in a Canadian town west of Winnipeg, I recalled, as a lad, pausing at the monument erected on the main street of the town, and reading the names engraved in marble. As I stood in reverence reading the names of those who had died in conflict, older men of the village would pat my head and say softly, "These, son, are the names of those who died to make your world safe. They died that no more would ever have to die in battle." How wrong they proved to be. With the passing of time, wars not only became more frequent, but weapons more destructive.

Futile Quest for Peace

Rivers of ink and acres of paper would be required to record man's futile quest for peace. In the thirteenth century, the wild horsemen of Genghis Khan swept out of Mongolia across the steppes of Central Asia, and burned the capital Kiev. The Tatar yoke lasted 240 years. The Russians have never forgotten the rule that finally ended in 1480. The pages of history reveal that Russia has been at war 75% of the time during the past seven centuries. France and Britain have been involved in wars over 50% of the last seven centuries. In 3,358 years of man's history, he could point to only 227 years of global peace. From 1500 B.C. to A.D. 1860, man had signed 8,000 treaties — with an average life expectancy of less than two years.

A Norwegian statistician goes even further and says that in 5,560 years of history, man has fought 14,531 wars. This represents 2.6 wars per year. In 885 generations, we have witnessed only *10 years* of unsullied peace. More than 600 million men have marched to the battlefields of the world never to return.

13

Man Loses Hope
in Man

IN GOD WE TRUST. So widespread and deep
was that conviction in the American colonies that the
founding fathers never even thought twice before affixing
it to the coin of the realm. There was no doubt in their
minds as to who *the* Founding Father was, to whom they
owed everything, and whose advice and consent they invariably sought before making any federal, local, or personal decision.

But somewhere along the way, with the dawn of the
scientific revolution and the Age of Reason, with its unprecedented affluence, we began to think that we *had done*
it ourselves, that we *could* do it ourselves. More and more
intellectuals and teachers were assuring us that God did
not exist, that with the elevation of man's mind, even the
concept of God was no longer essential.

And for those of us who did not already know Him, this
suited our emerging frame of mind, as we made idols of
self-reliance, self-confidence — self-centeredness. Look at
all *we* have accomplished; see what *we* can do.

And the scientists and the planners, flush with the first-
fruits of the new technology, said, "Come to us with all
your problems. Given enough time and goodwill, there is

nothing we cannot solve." But somehow there was never enough time, and goodwill was little more than a Christmas-card sentiment, and for every problem they sought to solve, they seemed to create ten more that no one had been able to foresee.

And now, as the voices of the increasingly disillusioned are raised against them, they eschew the enormous responsibility they once so lightly assumed, retorting, "Well, we're not God, are we?" No, they are not. But they were more than willing to be in the beginning.

So man has come to the end of his resources. He has risked everything on his ability to do it himself, and all he has succeeded in doing is pulling his world down around his ears. In the enormity of what he has done, at last he is beginning to see that in his own strength he can do nothing.

The result? For some, a turning back to the God once trusted, and a joyous rediscovery that He never changed. He can be absolutely trusted yesterday, today, and forever.

But for the majority, utter despair—on a scale the world has never known. Hedonism, hatred of morality, mindless violence—and amongst our youth, bitter rejection of authority and a blaming of "those in charge" for the hopeless mess the world is in. And escape—into alcohol, drugs, Eastern mind religions, anything to get as far away from reality as possible. But there is no permanent escape, save one.

It has been estimated that one thousand American college students will succeed in taking their own lives this year, nine thousand will attempt suicide, and ninety thousand will threaten to take their lives. And further, that one hundred young people attempt suicide for every one that is officially recorded. The despair at the degenerating world seems to be reflected even in the lives of some of the smaller children. On the front page of the Los Angeles

Herald Examiner, there appeared a story. It read as follows:

> A gruesome little ditty called "Suicide Song" intended as a parody for a Parent-Teachers' Association skit was briefly Number One on the third grade Hit Parade in the Beach Community's schools. Teachers were aghast when they heard the words:
>
> > "Oh, come with me to the kitchen,
> > to the kitchen, to the kitchen.
> > Oh, come with me to the kitchen
> > and there a date with death we both will keep.
> > Turn on the gas in the oven,
> > in the oven, in the oven.
> > It will gently lull us both to sleep.
> > Listen to the hissing sound.
> > Listen to the hissing sound.
> > They are calling, gently calling you and me.
> > Listen to the hissing sound.
> > Listen to the hissing sound.
> > We'll say good-bye and die in ecstasy."
>
> It was sung to the tune of "Listen to the Mocking Bird."

While some American children sang such songs of tragedy, across the other side of the ocean in the USSR, school children were singing, "The Blight of the World Is Jesus."

The Source of Earth's Sorrow

What had happened to man's world? Why did he find himself in the enlightenment of intellectualism stumbling in the darkness of his own confusion with morals too low and taxes too high, power groups arrogant, crime rampant, and extremists violent? With his ability to put a billion characters a second on the computer tape, man had succeeded also in generalizing humanity — identity was stifled and individuals had been transformed into IBM cards. The environment of violence had become natural. Man had changed his world into a psychedelic asylum.

Where was the utopia that was to have been born of Hegel's dialectic triads? Marx and Engels had embraced the words of Hegel who wrote that the individual exists only for the state, the state is divine, the absolute end, the true God, the divinity which enjoys an authority and majesty absolute. Marx and Engels echoed in their *Manifesto* the writings of Kant who began with man rather than God and was followed by Nietzsche who presented the *Übermensch* or "Superman." These doctrines had not only filled the hearts of millions of the lower levels of society, they had been echoed time and again in the halls of the Security Council and the General Assembly of the UN even by the highest leaders of the world bodies. *Newsweek* published an interview with U Thant in which he said,

> I believe in the philosophy of thesis, antithesis and synthesis. From its present antithesis, I believe the world is moving toward a new synthesis.

Those who knew the basic philosophy and doctrine of Communism heard in these words the words of Hegel, Engels, and Karl Marx.

But any honest man could see that something was sadly lacking. The words of the world leaders reminded the listener of those spoken long ago by Cicero, who read the *Phaedo* and sighingly said,

> Plato . . . thou reasonest well, but —

From the days of Cicero and Plato to the present leaders like U Thant there remains the one problem word . . . "BUT"

A world of plenty and a day of peace so near, so possible
... "BUT" ....

The truth is our world *is* a world of plenty. The world's
finest scientists estimate earth's real riches to be her grain
and her gold, her fruit and gems, her timber and treasures
almost limitless in minerals and resources. Some suggest
that earth's combined wealth would conservatively total
one decillion dollars. Divide this equally among earth's
present population and every man, woman, and child would
be a billionaire a billion times over.

Divide the 58 million square miles of land equally and
every person alive today would have 10 acres each.

Many good men today dream and discuss a world that
man could live in if he were free from wars and deception
and self-destruction.

Dr. Peter Goldmark, who was President and Research
Director of CBS Laboratories for 36 years, shows for example how a hundred million Americans could build model
communities of 3000, and use only 4% of America's land.

R. Buckminster Fuller, is called by U. Thant, one of the
greatest philosopher-scientists of our time.

On April 26th, 1973, when flying from Dallas to Los
Angeles, I picked up the airline magazine and read in the
American Way the interview between the architect, Michael
Ben Eli and Buckminster Fuller. Mr. Fuller said,

> Sadly we see enormous numbers of stranded poverty-
> stricken people while potential abundance is being
> deliberately curtailed by governments subservient to
> the landlord's will.

> Humanity is so accustomed to failure it still assumes
> failure to be normal, and does not realize that it has
> literally earned — and actually acquired — the capability
> to take care of everyone on earth at a higher standard
> of living than ever heretofore experienced by anyone.

The really big fact is that we are going to have to go through a complete mental resorting of what it is all about. Then we are going to have to go about taking care of everybody not as on relief, but with the same spontaneous welcome and love accorded a new-born baby.

Landlordism will no longer be able to extract a ransom. *Money too will become obsolete,* with the ability to produce enough to take care of all.

The fact that we now have the capability to support all life and are not doing so means we have to introduce a *new* system. One that can make the world work.

The flight time between Dallas and Los Angeles was devoted primarily to the consideration of the words of Buckminster Fuller. It was not my first introduction to this philosopher-scientist. In past occasions our paths had crossed in American cities where each of us had been speaking under different auspices. I agreed with his conviction that the world was large enough and sufficiently rich to sustain all men on the highest level, under ideal conditions. But I could not agree that man alone, without God, could ever realize its potential.

After reading the "Master Plan for Living" provided by Peter Goldmark, and studying the blueprint for the future drawn by Buckminster Fuller, I had to sigh with Cicero and say . . . "Thou reasonest well . . . but"

Something was missing. I knew it, they knew it, all the leaders of the world knew it. The Kremlin was confused. The U.S. Senate was perplexed. The leaders of Europe were distressed. What was man's future, his ultimate end?

Distress with Perplexity

When disciples long ago discussed with Christ the conditions that would climax this age, He said there would be

Upon the earth distress of nations, with perplexity.

(Luke 21:25)

The Greek word for "distress" is *aporia,* meaning "unable to discover a way out" or "coming to an impasse."

The prophecies of the Bible, indeed, portray every detail that we could visualize in this present hour, but do not leave us in the valley of doom or in the darkness of the present moment. In discussing these days, Jesus added with a triumphant note,

And when these things begin to come to pass, then look up, and lift up your heads; for your redemption draweth nigh.

(Luke 21:28)

Surely the prophets of old promised God would come to man's side in the hour of his darkest trial. The day would dawn when His Son would sweep away the failures of the past centuries and establish law and order and usher in a kingdom of peace. But man still had not reached that moment when he was willing to lift his eyes and look up. No, he would still continue on the spiraling downward pathway of human failure.

In the famous conversation between Raymond Swing and Albert Einstein, Mr. Swing said,

Either we will find a way to establish world government, or we will perish in a war of the atom.

Doctor Einstein replied,

The secret of the bomb should be committed to a world government, and the USA should immediately announce its readiness to give it to a world government.

Commenting on this 1945 exchange, Sumner Wells, in *The Atomic Bomb and World Government,* wrote,

No world government of the character envisaged by Professor Einstein would function unless it possessed the power to exercise complete control over the armaments of each constituent state.

As men began to move more rapidly toward world government, fear was expressed by some of the world's finest intellectuals. Doctor Charles Merriam, for many years professor of political economy in the University of Chicago, said,

I raise my voice to warn — human liberty may be lost.

But most intellectuals were not only willing to concede that liberty would be lost, they were in favor of disposing of it. Professor Laski of Oxford, England, declared,

Sovereignty must go; that means also the interests which sovereignty protects must be recognized as outmoded in character and dangerous in operation.

As I moved from country to country I was astonished at the amazing political phenomena of the times, the continued trend toward totalitarian controls. A world government of unprecedented size and power would still of necessity demand a world leader. Men had reached the place where they were not only willing to accept such a suggestion, but were willing to cry for strong individual leadership in this hour.

Few men expressed themselves more firmly in this respect than Paul Henri Spaak. A European statesman born in Brussels, Spaak led the Socialist Party of Belgium and was the first president of the Council of Europe. One of the planners of the European Common Market, he also served as president of the United Nations' General Assembly and as Secretary-General of NATO. In addition, he served as Prime Minister of Belgium and as Minister of Foreign Affairs for his country. Few men had filled such a roster of important offices. Spaak repeatedly expressed his desire to see a strong man arise on the world horizon to lead men out of the confusion of their present dilemma:

Let that man be a military man or a layman, it matters not.

Spaak's cry for strong one-man rule was echoed on the lips of many leaders. Roswell Gilpatric, former Deputy Secretary of Defense, said,

Strong, one-man civilian control of America's giant military establishment is vital to the nation's well-being. The concentration of authority is inevitable.

Crisis Measures

In America, at the time of the Cuban Missile Crisis in 1962, a series of emergency measures were formulated, to be followed in the event of a full confrontation, and they were signed into law by the late John F. Kennedy. They stand today exactly as they were signed on February 16 and February 27, 1962. Those emergency documents provide that the president should have complete and final dictatorial control, the authority to undertake immediate and decisive action. His executive orders are to be carried out through the Office of Emergency Planning and they are to be put into effect,

in any time of increased international tension or economic or financial crisis.

These orders are all-inclusive:

Executive Order 10995 — to take over all communication media.
Executive Order 10997 — take over all electric power, petroleum, gas, fuels, and minerals.

Executive Order 10998 — take over all food resources and farms.

Executive Order 10999 — take over all methods of transportation, highways, and seaports.

Executive Order 11000 — mobilization of civilians and work forces under governmental supervision.

Executive Order 11001 — take over all health, welfare, and educational functions.

Executive Order 11002 — the Postmaster-General, a member of the President's Cabinet, will operate a nationwide registration of all persons.

Executive Order 11003 — to take over all airports and aircraft.

Executive Order 11004 — take over housing and finance authorities — to relocate communities — to build new housing with public funds — designate areas to be abandoned as unsafe — establish new locations for populations.

Executive Order 11005 — take over all railroads, inland waterways, and public storage facilities.

Executive Order 11051 — designate responsibilities of Office of Emergency Planning, give authorization to put all other executive orders in effect in times of increased international tension or economic or financial crises.

The word "crisis" seemed to be appearing almost weekly in the headlines of the news media — population crisis, war crisis, fuel and energy crisis. If man was willing under crisis to commit total and absolute power to an individual leader of the nation or the world, how sudden and complete could be the revolutionary new methods swept in by such a man!

Who could administer such an instant world government?

H. G. Wells expressed the sentiments of millions when he wrote,

> It is necessary to discover a head capable of directing it, endowed with an intelligence surpassing the most elevated human level.

Over and over I found myself quoting those statements of Wells — "endowed with an intelligence surpassing the most elevated human level . . . surpassing the most elevated human level."

The Leader

Did Wells actually visualize a world leader with supernatural power? If so, from whom would such a ruler receive his power? Were there other men as prominent as Wells who entertained similar thoughts? I soon discovered that there were.

A recent poll in U.S.A. revealed that over 60% of the population believed in supernatural powers outside the human realm.

In May of 1973, *Reader's Digest* featured an article on page 255 relating to the discovery of life in outer space. It suggested that the scientific pendulum since 1963 had been swinging toward the side of evidence of life beyond the boundaries of our planet.

I recalled the words of the Astronomer Gibson Reeves who referred to "a rebelling mind somewhere in the universe having its effect on our planet earth. I wondered when I read the words of Gibson Reeves, if he was referring to Lucifer who long ago, according to the prophets of the Bible, led a rebellion in his desire to be equal with Christ.

Again I pondered the words of Isaiah who wrote,

> How art thou fallen from heaven, O Lucifer, son of the morning! — For thou hast said in thine heart, I

will ascend into heaven – I will be like the most high.

(Isa. 14:12–14)

John, Jude and Peter, Ezekiel and Isaiah all wrote concerning the rebellion led by Lucifer. The prophets defined the cause of his rebellion, named the number that followed him and described his ultimate destruction. Of utmost importance was the effect this had on men on earth.

On November 16, 1972, Pope Paul VI, addressing an audience of 6,000 people said,

We are all under an obscure domination. It is by Satan, the prince of this world.

Dr. Billy Graham addressing thousands said,

The devil is very real. Everyone knows that there are supernatural powers in the world.

One might expect Dr. Graham or Pope Paul to believe in Satan, but references to Lucifer or Satan were beginning to appear more frequently in unexpected places.

I recalled a sleepless night in the Admiral Benbow Inn, in Memphis, Tenn. It was not bad food nor a bad dream which kept me awake, it was a volume published by Encyclopedia Britannica entitled *Great Ideas of 1971*.

Much of the volume was devoted to the words of men who wrote in favor of World Government. I weighed carefully their comments and compared particularly the blueprint drawn by Dr. Hutchinson and his committee to the description of world government written by the prophet John almost 2000 years earlier. I was fascinated at the similarities.

Suddenly I came to page 118 and stared with amazement at what I read. From book 5, Chapter 5, quotations were printed from Dostoevsky's *The Brothers Karamazov*. Here the Russian writer depicted Jesus returning to earth, being rejected by a world leader who said,

Why hast Thou come now to hinder us? . . . We are working not with Thee but with him (Satan) . . . We took from him what Thou didst reject with scorn, that last gift he offered Thee, showing Thee all the kingdoms of the earth. We took from him Rome and the sword of Caesar, and proclaimed ourselves sole rulers of the earth . . . We shall triumph and shall be Caesars, and then we shall plan the universal happiness of man . . . Hadst Thou accepted that last counsel of the mighty spirit (Satan), Thou wouldst have accomplished all that man seeks on earth — that is, someone to worship . . . Who can rule men if not he who holds their conscience and their bread in his hands?

And I recalled those haunting words in the Gospel of Luke:

And the devil taking him [Jesus] up into an high mountain, shewed unto him all the kingdoms of the world in a moment of time. And the devil said unto him, All this power will I give thee, and the glory of them: for that is delivered unto me; and to whomsoever I will I give it. If thou therefore wilt worship me, all shall be thine. And Jesus answered and said unto him, Get thee behind me, Satan: for it is written, Thou shalt worship the Lord thy God, and Him only shalt thou serve."   (Luke 4:5–8)

Jesus did not bow down to Satan, but neither did He discount Satan's claim to the glories of this world when he said, "That is delivered unto me; and to whomsoever I will I give it."

No, Christ did not refute the claim of Lucifer that the glories of earth had been delivered unto him, nor did he deny that he could give the same to any who would follow or worship him.

Christ referred to him as The Prince of this World. (John 14:30)

Somewhere apparently in the distant past Lucifer had been given a certain authority over the planet Earth.

One day, according to the prophets of the Bible, his jurisdiction over earth would end and he would be judged and destroyed.

No one knew this better than Lucifer himself. The prophet John says,

He hath great wrath because he knoweth that he hath but a short time. (Rev. 12:12)

The aspiration which prompted him to lead his first rebellion was the desire to be like the Most High who was worshiped.

Lucifer longed to be worshiped. He offered Christ the power and glory of earth in exchange for just one thing . . . His worship.

The words of Dostoevsky were much more than foolish fiction. They resembled all too literally the words of the prophet John who declared in the 13th Chapter of Revelation that Lucifer would give his wisdom and power to those who would be leaders of the final form of government in which sinful man would rule the world.

The prophet John however does not conclude his message as Dostoevsky does. John agrees that men of Satanic power will hold world authority for a brief time, but that they will be overthrown by Christ who will establish righteousness and universal peace and order.

This final act will be the glorious climax, the grand finale of all that has been written by the prophets. The book of Revelation closes in a blaze of glory where truth triumphs and men live in a New Earth wherein dwelleth righteousness.

The log on the hearth had almost turned to ashes. Only
a few red embers still lingered on the grate. The night hours
had virtually slipped away, and I shivered a little, as I
stirred the last of the coals with an effort to encourage them
to one final flame.

What scenes had unfolded before me in that fire during
those night hours of reverie and meditation!

The battle of the ages had been reenacted before my
eyes. The symbolic dove of peace had not yet found a resting place on earth, nor would it until the Prince of Peace
would come. But the hour was drawing near. I could see
the rosy rays of promise breaking over the pages of the
inspired writings of the prophets who said,

"He that shall come will come, and will not tarry."
(Heb. 10:37)

If a thousand inspired utterances penned in the past had
already been miraculously fulfilled, the few remaining
prophecies would surely be fulfilled as well.

Lucifer's rebellion against God had continued through
the centuries. Men on earth had also been included in a
conflict which seemed endless.

The story of this struggle had been written with the ink
of blood and tears. The concluding chapter was now being
penned.

The final scene of battle would be in the Middle East.
According to the prophet Ezekiel, Russia and her allies
would march against Israel. He writes:

And thou shalt come up against my people of Israel,
as a cloud to cover the land; it shall be in the latter
days.   (Ezekiel 38:16)

How little do the Russian leaders know the destruction
that awaits them in their coming invasion of Israel! They
have for many years opposed the church, oppressed the

Jews and hurled insults in the face of God and His Son. I had seen posters produced by the anti-God artists of Communism depicting the working-man dumping Jesus Christ in a sewer, and others mocking the sacrament showing men eating the dismembered body of Jesus in a suggested orgy of cannibalism.

God is not ignorant of the insults and attacks made against Him and His followers by the leaders of Communism who cry "We hate all gods." There is a day of reckoning coming, and God's prophets tell how, when and where it will take place.

The prophet Ezekiel who sees Russia in the latter days turning her face toward Israel writes,

> Thus saith the Lord God; It shall come to pass, that at the same time shall things come into thy mind, and thou shalt think an evil thought: And thou shalt say, I will go . . . To take a spoil.   (Ezekiel 38:10–12)

No where in the world is there greater spoil than the oil of the Middle East.

In Saudi Arabia alone, Ahmed Zaki Yamani, Minister of Oil, estimates their reserves at 150 billion barrels which is 30% of the world's known reserves. Some estimate that in less than seven years the oil of the Middle East could represent as much as $250 billion in value.

There is also the wealth of the Dead Sea with its limitless deposits of potash and other chemicals. Added to all of this is the importance of the Middle East geographically. Some have crudely but aptly referred to the Middle East, in the center of the globe as "the jugular vein of the World."

If Lucifer declared he would grant the riches of earth to those who would follow him, this promise should surely apply to the anti-God leaders of Communism.

Little do the atheistic armies of Russia realize as they march toward Palestine, that they are marching toward their own destruction. Lucifer's reign as Prince of this

World is about to end. His time has finally run out. The prophet Ezekiel tells how God views this final act and says,

> Thus saith the Lord God; in that day when my people of Israel dwelleth safely, shalt thou not know it? And thou shalt come from thy place out of the north parts — a great company, and a mighty army: And thou shalt come against my people of Israel, as a cloud to cover the land; it shall be in the latter days.
> (Ezekiel 38:14–16)

Two verses later, the prophet describes God's fury and in verse 22, he tells of the fire from heaven that destroys the armies of Russia and her allies.

As I studied these stupendous statements, I found myself wondering whether the destruction of the Russian armies was caused by an atomic holocaust or by Divine intervention. Perhaps, I said to myself, it was each.

As I read on into the next chapter, one thing was extremely clear, God had declared His opposition to this invasion and through the pen of His prophet wrote,

> And I will turn thee back, and leave but a sixth part of thee — and seven months shall the house of Israel be burying of them.   (Ezek. 39:2 and 12).

No, I said slowly, God is neither unjust nor unmerciful. He cannot allow Lucifer to succeed in this final act of aggression, nor can He allow those who follow the Prince of this World to triumph in their march against Israel and gain world control.

World control? Ah, yes, that has been the dream and desire of Lucifer through all of the ages. Follow me! he cried, Obey me! Worship me! Ye shall be as Gods, and the glories of this world shall be thine.

Among those willing to follow Lucifer were the money

changers whose God was Mammon. Though Christ drove them from the temple, they did not disappear from earth. The Luciferian Society of money changers became the unseen rulers over kings and princes.

The cry of the dying soldiers and the blood of a hundred battlefields meant nothing to those who saw an opportunity to gain wealth through war.

How clear, I said slowly, how very clear is the strategy of Lucifer when explained by the prophets of the Bible. He deceives the world leaders and leads them to the battlefields to fight wars which cost billions of dollars to fight. To obtain the vast sums of money essential to waging wars, the governments of the world were forced to borrow from the moneylenders who were the High Priests of Finance. On these astronomical war debts the taxpayers were forced to pay interest.

Presently, the annual cost of arms and armies demanded payments equalling all of the paychecks of one-third of the world's poorer people. With the arms race continuing unabated, a spokesman for the U.N. predicted an annual price tag of a trillion dollars by 1980. Nations would continue to sink deeper in debt, and taxpayers would continue to pay interest to international bankers, who according to Dr. Quigley,

> were different from ordinary bankers and were concerned with questions of government debts. They were devoted to secrecy and financial influence in political life.

I thought on these words and repeated again the words written by Curtis B. Dall concerning the international bankers when he wrote,

> They are driving toward complete control of the world's long-range monetary policy — for their own profit. They foment foreign wars to aid this objective.

The objective? Yes, the objective of those gaining control of the world's wealth was to have total authority over all mankind.

My thoughts turned one more time to the writings of the Russian Dostoevsky who said,

> We shall triumph—we shall plan the universal happiness of man.

This, said Dostoevsky, would be accomplished by the one who would hold control of man's conscience and his bread.

The only happiness sought by Lucifer, however, was not man's good but his own Satanic desire to have men worship him. If he controlled man's bread he could force men to bow to him.

The prophet John tells how this world leader who will have power over "all kindreds and tongues and nations" (Rev. 13:7) will cause that as many as will not worship—shall be killed. (Rev. 13:15).

And again I recalled the fantastic passage of scripture that I had repeated so many times before,

> He causeth all small and great, rich and poor, free and bond, to receive a mark in their right hand or in their foreheads: and that no man might buy or sell save he that had the mark—or the number.
>
> (Rev. 13:16–17)

This would seem to be Lucifer's hour of triumph. He has struggled many long centuries to reach this goal. He has deceived the nations in leading them to battle. He has imparted his cunning and power to the money changers of the world who have stripped the masses of their wealth and have brought all mankind under a number system.

Now, he cries, men must worship me or be put to death. No man can buy or sell or live in my one-world society, unless he takes the number of our universe.

I had seen wars bring debts and rationing. I had seen certain natural circumstances contribute to the establishment of the International Monetary Fund and the World Bank. I had witnessed the computer age transform our world into IBM cards where men were filed as digits rather than people. I had viewed the skylines of the world's leading cities, where bank buildings rose heavenward like giant cathedrals.

Unbelievable, I said, as I studied these superstructures dominating the horizons of the world. Unbelievable that some of these great banking houses will be devoid of vaults. They will have no need of such, for in place of money will be only computers which carry a man's number and determine his allowance in a world-wide ration system.

Even while I thought on these truths, I was moved with the knowledge that banking houses were perfecting the non-toxic ink with which a number could be implanted for life on man's flesh.

The world system will be praised and promoted by brilliant men. With eloquence and apparent logic they will persuade men that this is the path to peace and security.

The world leader will rise to power with flattery and gain complete control of the military and monetary powers of all nations.

A dark picture? Yes, indeed. But hardly the conclusion of man's drama.

John the revelator did not conclude his book called Revelation with the universal number system described in Chapter 13, nor the battle of Armageddon in Chapter 16, nor the anti-Christ system under Lucifer mentioned in Chapters 17 through 19. Thank God, the prophet John writes Chapter 20 describing the overthrow of Lucifer and his forces diabolic. Chapters 20 and 21 describe with inspired eloquence a new heaven and earth, where blood no longer is shed, where tears no longer flow, where war clouds no longer darken the sky.

The glorious daybreak of deliverance dawning on a world which had suffered for so many centuries the deception and destruction brought to earth by Lucifer the archenemy of God and man.

When Christ was on earth as the Savior of men, Lucifer sought to tempt Him by offering Him earth's glories. He knew Christ had come for one express purpose described by John who wrote,

For this purpose the Son of God was manifested, that He might destroy the works of the devil."

(1 John 3:8)

Satan recognized Christ as the Son of God even when men looked on Him only as the carpenter's son. Lucifer cried,

I know who thou art Jesus thou son of the most High God. Hast thou come to torment me before the time?

Lucifer knew that Christ had said, "I will come again" (John 14:3) "Ye shall see the Son of Man sitting on the right hand of power." (Mark 16:42).

Jude also writes, and Enoch, the seventh from Adam, prophesied: the Lord cometh to execute judgement upon all. (Jude 14).

When doing a documentary film on the United Nations, I paused outside the U.N. and gazed with incredulity at the huge marble slab on which had been engraved a message from the USSR.

It was a quotation from the prophet Isaiah pertaining to the return of Christ. Some read this and asked if some miracle had caused the atheistic leaders of Communism to acknowledge their own failures and the world's only hope in the return of Christ, when they chiseled in marble for the world to read,

"and they shall beat their swords into ploughshares, and their spears into pruning hooks; nation shall not

lift sword against nation neither shall they learn war
any more."   (Isa. 2:4).

The presentation of scripture by the Communists to the
UN was really no miracle, but merely another example of
deception. When Lucifer tempted Christ, he, too, quoted
scripture—broken scripture and half-truth, scripture taken
out of context.

The words chiseled in marble by the Communists spoke
of universal peace, but the inference was a peace brought
to man by the UN, not by God.

If the Communist leaders had presented to the UN a
plaque bearing the complete scripture written by Isaiah
rather than a half-truth, it would have commenced with the
statement,

> and it shall come to pass in the last days, that the
> mountains of the Lord's house shall be established—
> and many people shall go and say—we will walk in
> His paths.
> . . . and He shall judge among the nations and shall
> rebuke many people: (Isaiah 2:2–4)

and concluded with the words,

> and let us walk in the light of the Lord.   (Isa. 2:5)

The prophet Micah penned words identical to Isaiah
and added the glorious statements,

> And they shall sit every man under his vine and under
> his fig tree; and none shall make him afraid; for the
> mouth of the Lord of hosts hath spoken it . . .
>
> and we will walk in the name of the Lord our God for
> ever and ever.   (Micah 4:4–5)

This indeed is the glorious truth that all the prophets of
the Bible emphasize. The prophet Daniel speaks of the
hour when

The God of Heaven shall set up a kingdom which
shall never be destroyed; and the kingdom shall not
be left to other people – it shall stand forever.

(Daniel 2:44)

But what will it take to deliver man from the greed and
lust and hatred which flow from sinful hearts? God's word
declares it will take the final and complete destruction of
Lucifer and his legions, which through the centuries have
blinded the minds of men even as the Apostle Paul declares
(II Cor. 4:4).

When Lord Gladstone was Prime Minister of England,
he said,

More and more I find my thoughts turning to the great
statement – when the Son of Man cometh.

This indeed is man's great hope. I sat in the heart of
London with one of Britain's brilliant writers, Kenneth
DeCoursey, and he told of a conversation with Winston
Churchill who referred to the return of Christ as man's
only hope.

It is indeed a hope that soon will be fulfilled. Man need
not, however, wait only for the physical return of Christ to
overthrow the Kingdom of Evil. His Spirit, which is already
in the world, will enter the heart of everyone willing to
bow humbly in recognizing Him as Lord and Master.

Christ not only spoke of his coming Kingdom, He also
declared that the Kingdom of God can be within you. This
is not only a privilege, *it is imperative* if one will inhabit the
Kingdom to come.

Christ said to Nicodemus,

Except a man be born again he cannot see the Kingdom of God.   (John 3:3)

These words sounded strange to the ruler of the Jews,
and he asked how could these things be? But the mystery

did not hinder him from accepting by faith the realities of the spiritual kingdom which would lead him into the literal kingdom of God.

One day, Christ will reign as Lord and Master on the throne of every heart, and Righteousness will cover the earth as the waters cover the sea.

I turned to the window with amazement and realized the sun was now breaking on the eastern horizon. The birds were singing in the light of dawn; the world was awakening to a new day. The last glowing embers had died on the hearth; the hours of the night had passed. I walked to the front door, threw it open, and stepping outside, I faced the sun. Prophecy, I cried, is truly a light in a dark place. Even in the shadows of the present confusion we have, as Peter declared, a sure word of prophecy:

> Where unto ye do well that ye take heed, as unto a light that shineth in a dark place, until the day dawns, and the day star arise in your hearts. (II Peter 1:19)

Correspondence regarding the author's personal ministry should be addressed to:

Willard Cantelon
Box 10010
Glendale, California 91209